ISBN 0-8373-0635-3

C-635 CAREER EXAMINATION SERIES

This is your PASSBOOK® for...

Public Relations Assistant

Test Preparation Study Guide

Questions & Answers

EAST NORTHPORT PUBLIC LIBRARY
EAST NORTHPORT, NEW YORK

NATIONAL LEARNING CORPORATION

Copyright © 2015 by

National Learning Corporation
212 Michael Drive, Syosset, New York 11791

All rights reserved, including the right of reproduction in whole or in part, in any form or by any means, electronic or mechanical, including photocopying, recording, or by any information storage and retrieval system, without permission in writing from the Publisher.

(516) 921-8888
(800) 645-6337
FAX: (516) 921-8743
www.passbooks.com
sales @ passbooks.com
info @ passbooks.com

PRINTED IN THE UNITED STATES OF AMERICA

PASSBOOK®
NOTICE

This book is SOLELY intended for, is sold ONLY to, and its use is RESTRICTED to *individual*, bona fide applicants or candidates who qualify by virtue of having seriously filed applications for appropriate license, certificate, professional and/or promotional advancement, higher school matriculation, scholarship, or other legitimate requirements of educational and/or governmental authorities.

This book is NOT intended for use, class instruction, tutoring, training, duplication, copying, reprinting, excerption, or adaptation, etc., by:

(1) Other publishers

(2) Proprietors and/or Instructors of "Coaching" and/or Preparatory Courses

(3) Personnel and/or Training Divisions of commercial, industrial, and governmental organizations

(4) Schools, colleges, or universities and/or their departments and staffs, including teachers and other personnel

(5) Testing Agencies or Bureaus

(6) Study groups which seek by the purchase of a single volume to copy and/or duplicate and/or adapt this material for use by the group as a whole without having purchased individual volumes for each of the members of the group

(7) Et al.

Such persons would be in violation of appropriate Federal and State statutes.

PROVISION OF LICENSING AGREEMENTS. — Recognized educational commercial, industrial, and governmental institutions and organizations, and others legitimately engaged in educational pursuits, including training, testing, and measurement activities, may address a request for a licensing agreement to the copyright owners, who will determine whether, and under what conditions, including fees and charges, the materials in this book may be used by them. In other words, a licensing facility exists for the legitimate use of the material in this book on other than an individual basis. However, it is asseverated and affirmed here that the material in this book *CANNOT* be used without the receipt of the express permission of such a licensing agreement from the Publishers.

NATIONAL LEARNING CORPORATION
212 Michael Drive
Syosset, New York 11791

Inquiries re licensing agreements should be addressed to:
The President
National Learning Corporation
212 Michael Drive
Syosset, New York 11791

PASSBOOK® SERIES

THE *PASSBOOK® SERIES* has been created to prepare applicants and candidates for the ultimate academic battlefield – the examination room.

At some time in our lives, each and every one of us may be required to take an examination – for validation, matriculation, admission, qualification, registration, certification, or licensure.

Based on the assumption that every applicant or candidate has met the basic formal educational standards, has taken the required number of courses, and read the necessary texts, the *PASSBOOK® SERIES* furnishes the one special preparation which may assure passing with confidence, instead of failing with insecurity. Examination questions – together with answers – are furnished as the basic vehicle for study so that the mysteries of the examination and its compounding difficulties may be eliminated or diminished by a sure method.

This book is meant to help you pass your examination provided that you qualify and are serious in your objective.

The entire field is reviewed through the huge store of content information which is succinctly presented through a provocative and challenging approach – the question-and-answer method.

A climate of success is established by furnishing the correct answers at the end of each test.

You soon learn to recognize types of questions, forms of questions, and patterns of questioning. You may even begin to anticipate expected outcomes.

You perceive that many questions are repeated or adapted so that you can gain acute insights, which may enable you to score many sure points.

You learn how to confront new questions, or types of questions, and to attack them confidently and work out the correct answers.

You note objectives and emphases, and recognize pitfalls and dangers, so that you may make positive educational adjustments.

Moreover, you are kept fully informed in relation to new concepts, methods, practices, and directions in the field.

You discover that you are actually taking the examination all the time: you are preparing for the examination by "taking" an examination, not by reading extraneous and/or supererogatory textbooks.

In short, this PASSBOOK®, used directedly, should be an important factor in helping you to pass your test.

PUBLIC RELATIONS ASSISTANT

DUTIES
Assists in conducting a public-relations program for an agency. Serves as a liaison between the agency, the general public and the news media. Answers inquiries, provides information, and clarifies the intentions and status of projects and services of the agency. Responsibility may also be included for receiving and handling complaints from the public. The incumbent is expected to use some judgment and initiative in performing duties. The work is performed under the supervision of an administrative superior and is reviewed through conferences and written reports. Performs related work as required.

SCOPE OF THE EXAMINATION
The written test will cover knowledge, skills and/or abilities in such areas as:

1. Educating and interacting with the public;
2. Grammar, usage, punctuation and editing;
3. Preparing written material; and
4. Understanding and interpreting written material.

HOW TO TAKE A TEST

I. YOU MUST PASS AN EXAMINATION

A. *WHAT EVERY CANDIDATE SHOULD KNOW*

Examination applicants often ask us for help in preparing for the written test. What can I study in advance? What kinds of questions will be asked? How will the test be given? How will the papers be graded?

As an applicant for a civil service examination, you may be wondering about some of these things. Our purpose here is to suggest effective methods of advance study and to describe civil service examinations.

Your chances for success on this examination can be increased if you know how to prepare. Those "pre-examination jitters" can be reduced if you know what to expect. You can even experience an adventure in good citizenship if you know why civil service exams are given.

B. *WHY ARE CIVIL SERVICE EXAMINATIONS GIVEN?*

Civil service examinations are important to you in two ways. As a citizen, you want public jobs filled by employees who know how to do their work. As a job seeker, you want a fair chance to compete for that job on an equal footing with other candidates. The best-known means of accomplishing this two-fold goal is the competitive examination.

Exams are widely publicized throughout the nation. They may be administered for jobs in federal, state, city, municipal, town or village governments or agencies.

Any citizen may apply, with some limitations, such as the age or residence of applicants. Your experience and education may be reviewed to see whether you meet the requirements for the particular examination. When these requirements exist, they are reasonable and applied consistently to all applicants. Thus, a competitive examination may cause you some uneasiness now, but it is your privilege and safeguard.

C. *HOW ARE CIVIL SERVICE EXAMS DEVELOPED?*

Examinations are carefully written by trained technicians who are specialists in the field known as "psychological measurement," in consultation with recognized authorities in the field of work that the test will cover. These experts recommend the subject matter areas or skills to be tested; only those knowledges or skills important to your success on the job are included. The most reliable books and source materials available are used as references. Together, the experts and technicians judge the difficulty level of the questions.

Test technicians know how to phrase questions so that the problem is clearly stated. Their ethics do not permit "trick" or "catch" questions. Questions may have been tried out on sample groups, or subjected to statistical analysis, to determine their usefulness.

Written tests are often used in combination with performance tests, ratings of training and experience, and oral interviews. All of these measures combine to form the best-known means of finding the right person for the right job.

II. HOW TO PASS THE WRITTEN TEST

A. NATURE OF THE EXAMINATION

To prepare intelligently for civil service examinations, you should know how they differ from school examinations you have taken. In school you were assigned certain definite pages to read or subjects to cover. The examination questions were quite detailed and usually emphasized memory. Civil service exams, on the other hand, try to discover your present ability to perform the duties of a position, plus your potentiality to learn these duties. In other words, a civil service exam attempts to predict how successful you will be. Questions cover such a broad area that they cannot be as minute and detailed as school exam questions.

In the public service similar kinds of work, or positions, are grouped together in one "class." This process is known as *position-classification*. All the positions in a class are paid according to the salary range for that class. One class title covers all of these positions, and they are all tested by the same examination.

B. FOUR BASIC STEPS

1) Study the announcement

How, then, can you know what subjects to study? Our best answer is: "Learn as much as possible about the class of positions for which you've applied." The exam will test the knowledge, skills and abilities needed to do the work.

Your most valuable source of information about the position you want is the official exam announcement. This announcement lists the training and experience qualifications. Check these standards and apply only if you come reasonably close to meeting them.

The brief description of the position in the examination announcement offers some clues to the subjects which will be tested. Think about the job itself. Review the duties in your mind. Can you perform them, or are there some in which you are rusty? Fill in the blank spots in your preparation.

Many jurisdictions preview the written test in the exam announcement by including a section called "Knowledge and Abilities Required," "Scope of the Examination," or some similar heading. Here you will find out specifically what fields will be tested.

2) Review your own background

Once you learn in general what the position is all about, and what you need to know to do the work, ask yourself which subjects you already know fairly well and which need improvement. You may wonder whether to concentrate on improving your strong areas or on building some background in your fields of weakness. When the announcement has specified "some knowledge" or "considerable knowledge," or has used adjectives like "beginning principles of…" or "advanced … methods," you can get a clue as to the number and difficulty of questions to be asked in any given field. More questions, and hence broader coverage, would be included for those subjects which are more important in the work. Now weigh your strengths and weaknesses against the job requirements and prepare accordingly.

3) Determine the level of the position

Another way to tell how intensively you should prepare is to understand the level of the job for which you are applying. Is it the entering level? In other words, is this the position in which beginners in a field of work are hired? Or is it an intermediate or advanced level? Sometimes this is indicated by such words as "Junior" or "Senior" in the class title. Other jurisdictions use Roman numerals to designate the level – Clerk I, Clerk II, for example. The word "Supervisor" sometimes appears in the title. If the level is not indicated by the title, check the description of duties. Will you be working under very close supervision, or will you have responsibility for independent decisions in this work?

4) Choose appropriate study materials

Now that you know the subjects to be examined and the relative amount of each subject to be covered, you can choose suitable study materials. For beginning level jobs, or even advanced ones, if you have a pronounced weakness in some aspect of your training, read a modern, standard textbook in that field. Be sure it is up to date and has general coverage. Such books are normally available at your library, and the librarian will be glad to help you locate one. For entry-level positions, questions of appropriate difficulty are chosen – neither highly advanced questions, nor those too simple. Such questions require careful thought but not advanced training.

If the position for which you are applying is technical or advanced, you will read more advanced, specialized material. If you are already familiar with the basic principles of your field, elementary textbooks would waste your time. Concentrate on advanced textbooks and technical periodicals. Think through the concepts and review difficult problems in your field.

These are all general sources. You can get more ideas on your own initiative, following these leads. For example, training manuals and publications of the government agency which employs workers in your field can be useful, particularly for technical and professional positions. A letter or visit to the government department involved may result in more specific study suggestions, and certainly will provide you with a more definite idea of the exact nature of the position you are seeking.

III. KINDS OF TESTS

Tests are used for purposes other than measuring knowledge and ability to perform specified duties. For some positions, it is equally important to test ability to make adjustments to new situations or to profit from training. In others, basic mental abilities not dependent on information are essential. Questions which test these things may not appear as pertinent to the duties of the position as those which test for knowledge and information. Yet they are often highly important parts of a fair examination. For very general questions, it is almost impossible to help you direct your study efforts. What we can do is to point out some of the more common of these general abilities needed in public service positions and describe some typical questions.

1) General information

Broad, general information has been found useful for predicting job success in some kinds of work. This is tested in a variety of ways, from vocabulary lists to questions about current events. Basic background in some field of work, such as sociology or economics, may be sampled in a group of questions. Often these are principles which have become familiar to most persons through exposure rather than through formal training. It is difficult to advise you how to study for these questions; being alert to the world around you is our best suggestion.

2) Verbal ability

An example of an ability needed in many positions is verbal or language ability. Verbal ability is, in brief, the ability to use and understand words. Vocabulary and grammar tests are typical measures of this ability. Reading comprehension or paragraph interpretation questions are common in many kinds of civil service tests. You are given a paragraph of written material and asked to find its central meaning.

3) Numerical ability

Number skills can be tested by the familiar arithmetic problem, by checking paired lists of numbers to see which are alike and which are different, or by interpreting charts and graphs. In the latter test, a graph may be printed in the test booklet which you are asked to use as the basis for answering questions.

4) Observation

A popular test for law-enforcement positions is the observation test. A picture is shown to you for several minutes, then taken away. Questions about the picture test your ability to observe both details and larger elements.

5) Following directions

In many positions in the public service, the employee must be able to carry out written instructions dependably and accurately. You may be given a chart with several columns, each column listing a variety of information. The questions require you to carry out directions involving the information given in the chart.

6) Skills and aptitudes

Performance tests effectively measure some manual skills and aptitudes. When the skill is one in which you are trained, such as typing or shorthand, you can practice. These tests are often very much like those given in business school or high school courses. For many of the other skills and aptitudes, however, no short-time preparation can be made. Skills and abilities natural to you or that you have developed throughout your lifetime are being tested.

Many of the general questions just described provide all the data needed to answer the questions and ask you to use your reasoning ability to find the answers. Your best preparation for these tests, as well as for tests of facts and ideas, is to be at your physical and mental best. You, no doubt, have your own methods of getting into an exam-taking mood and keeping "in shape." The next section lists some ideas on this subject.

IV. KINDS OF QUESTIONS

Only rarely is the "essay" question, which you answer in narrative form, used in civil service tests. Civil service tests are usually of the short-answer type. Full instructions for answering these questions will be given to you at the examination. But in case this is your first experience with short-answer questions and separate answer sheets, here is what you need to know:

1) Multiple-choice Questions

Most popular of the short-answer questions is the "multiple choice" or "best answer" question. It can be used, for example, to test for factual knowledge, ability to solve problems or judgment in meeting situations found at work.

A multiple-choice question is normally one of three types—
- It can begin with an incomplete statement followed by several possible endings. You are to find the one ending which *best* completes the statement, although some of the others may not be entirely wrong.
- It can also be a complete statement in the form of a question which is answered by choosing one of the statements listed.

- It can be in the form of a problem – again you select the best answer.

Here is an example of a multiple-choice question with a discussion which should give you some clues as to the method for choosing the right answer:

When an employee has a complaint about his assignment, the action which will *best* help him overcome his difficulty is to
- A. discuss his difficulty with his coworkers
- B. take the problem to the head of the organization
- C. take the problem to the person who gave him the assignment
- D. say nothing to anyone about his complaint

In answering this question, you should study each of the choices to find which is best. Consider choice "A" – Certainly an employee may discuss his complaint with fellow employees, but no change or improvement can result, and the complaint remains unresolved. Choice "B" is a poor choice since the head of the organization probably does not know what assignment you have been given, and taking your problem to him is known as "going over the head" of the supervisor. The supervisor, or person who made the assignment, is the person who can clarify it or correct any injustice. Choice "C" is, therefore, correct. To say nothing, as in choice "D," is unwise. Supervisors have and interest in knowing the problems employees are facing, and the employee is seeking a solution to his problem.

2) True/False Questions

The "true/false" or "right/wrong" form of question is sometimes used. Here a complete statement is given. Your job is to decide whether the statement is right or wrong.

SAMPLE: A roaming cell-phone call to a nearby city costs less than a non-roaming call to a distant city.

This statement is wrong, or false, since roaming calls are more expensive.

This is not a complete list of all possible question forms, although most of the others are variations of these common types. You will always get complete directions for answering questions. Be sure you understand *how* to mark your answers – ask questions until you do.

V. RECORDING YOUR ANSWERS

Computer terminals are used more and more today for many different kinds of exams.

For an examination with very few applicants, you may be told to record your answers in the test booklet itself. Separate answer sheets are much more common. If this separate answer sheet is to be scored by machine – and this is often the case – it is highly important that you mark your answers correctly in order to get credit.

An electronic scoring machine is often used in civil service offices because of the speed with which papers can be scored. Machine-scored answer sheets must be marked with a pencil, which will be given to you. This pencil has a high graphite content which responds to the electronic scoring machine. As a matter of fact, stray dots may register as answers, so do not let your pencil rest on the answer sheet while you are pondering the correct answer. Also, if your pencil lead breaks or is otherwise defective, ask for another.

Since the answer sheet will be dropped in a slot in the scoring machine, be careful not to bend the corners or get the paper crumpled.

The answer sheet normally has five vertical columns of numbers, with 30 numbers to a column. These numbers correspond to the question numbers in your test booklet. After each number, going across the page are four or five pairs of dotted lines. These short dotted lines have small letters or numbers above them. The first two pairs may also have a "T" or "F" above the letters. This indicates that the first two pairs only are to be used if the questions are of the true-false type. If the questions are multiple choice, disregard the "T" and "F" and pay attention only to the small letters or numbers.

Answer your questions in the manner of the sample that follows:

32. The largest city in the United States is
    A. Washington, D.C.
    B. New York City
    C. Chicago
    D. Detroit
    E. San Francisco

1) Choose the answer you think is best. (New York City is the largest, so "B" is correct.)
2) Find the row of dotted lines numbered the same as the question you are answering. (Find row number 32)
3) Find the pair of dotted lines corresponding to the answer. (Find the pair of lines under the mark "B.")
4) Make a solid black mark between the dotted lines.

VI. BEFORE THE TEST

Common sense will help you find procedures to follow to get ready for an examination. Too many of us, however, overlook these sensible measures. Indeed, nervousness and fatigue have been found to be the most serious reasons why applicants fail to do their best on civil service tests. Here is a list of reminders:

- Begin your preparation early – Don't wait until the last minute to go scurrying around for books and materials or to find out what the position is all about.
- Prepare continuously – An hour a night for a week is better than an all-night cram session. This has been definitely established. What is more, a night a week for a month will return better dividends than crowding your study into a shorter period of time.
- Locate the place of the exam – You have been sent a notice telling you when and where to report for the examination. If the location is in a different town or otherwise unfamiliar to you, it would be well to inquire the best route and learn something about the building.
- Relax the night before the test – Allow your mind to rest. Do not study at all that night. Plan some mild recreation or diversion; then go to bed early and get a good night's sleep.
- Get up early enough to make a leisurely trip to the place for the test – This way unforeseen events, traffic snarls, unfamiliar buildings, etc. will not upset you.
- Dress comfortably – A written test is not a fashion show. You will be known by number and not by name, so wear something comfortable.

- Leave excess paraphernalia at home – Shopping bags and odd bundles will get in your way. You need bring only the items mentioned in the official notice you received; usually everything you need is provided. Do not bring reference books to the exam. They will only confuse those last minutes and be taken away from you when in the test room.
- Arrive somewhat ahead of time – If because of transportation schedules you must get there very early, bring a newspaper or magazine to take your mind off yourself while waiting.
- Locate the examination room – When you have found the proper room, you will be directed to the seat or part of the room where you will sit. Sometimes you are given a sheet of instructions to read while you are waiting. Do not fill out any forms until you are told to do so; just read them and be prepared.
- Relax and prepare to listen to the instructions
- If you have any physical problem that may keep you from doing your best, be sure to tell the test administrator. If you are sick or in poor health, you really cannot do your best on the exam. You can come back and take the test some other time.

VII. AT THE TEST

The day of the test is here and you have the test booklet in your hand. The temptation to get going is very strong. Caution! There is more to success than knowing the right answers. You must know how to identify your papers and understand variations in the type of short-answer question used in this particular examination. Follow these suggestions for maximum results from your efforts:

1) Cooperate with the monitor

The test administrator has a duty to create a situation in which you can be as much at ease as possible. He will give instructions, tell you when to begin, check to see that you are marking your answer sheet correctly, and so on. He is not there to guard you, although he will see that your competitors do not take unfair advantage. He wants to help you do your best.

2) Listen to all instructions

Don't jump the gun! Wait until you understand all directions. In most civil service tests you get more time than you need to answer the questions. So don't be in a hurry. Read each word of instructions until you clearly understand the meaning. Study the examples, listen to all announcements and follow directions. Ask questions if you do not understand what to do.

3) Identify your papers

Civil service exams are usually identified by number only. You will be assigned a number; you must not put your name on your test papers. Be sure to copy your number correctly. Since more than one exam may be given, copy your exact examination title.

4) Plan your time

Unless you are told that a test is a "speed" or "rate of work" test, speed itself is usually not important. Time enough to answer all the questions will be provided, but this does not mean that you have all day. An overall time limit has been set. Divide the total time (in minutes) by the number of questions to determine the approximate time you have for each question.

5) Do not linger over difficult questions

If you come across a difficult question, mark it with a paper clip (useful to have along) and come back to it when you have been through the booklet. One caution if you do this – be sure to skip a number on your answer sheet as well. Check often to be sure that you have not lost your place and that you are marking in the row numbered the same as the question you are answering.

6) Read the questions

Be sure you know what the question asks! Many capable people are unsuccessful because they failed to *read* the questions correctly.

7) Answer all questions

Unless you have been instructed that a penalty will be deducted for incorrect answers, it is better to guess than to omit a question.

8) Speed tests

It is often better NOT to guess on speed tests. It has been found that on timed tests people are tempted to spend the last few seconds before time is called in marking answers at random – without even reading them – in the hope of picking up a few extra points. To discourage this practice, the instructions may warn you that your score will be "corrected" for guessing. That is, a penalty will be applied. The incorrect answers will be deducted from the correct ones, or some other penalty formula will be used.

9) Review your answers

If you finish before time is called, go back to the questions you guessed or omitted to give them further thought. Review other answers if you have time.

10) Return your test materials

If you are ready to leave before others have finished or time is called, take ALL your materials to the monitor and leave quietly. Never take any test material with you. The monitor can discover whose papers are not complete, and taking a test booklet may be grounds for disqualification.

VIII. EXAMINATION TECHNIQUES

1) Read the general instructions carefully. These are usually printed on the first page of the exam booklet. As a rule, these instructions refer to the timing of the examination; the fact that you should not start work until the signal and must stop work at a signal, etc. If there are any *special* instructions, such as a choice of questions to be answered, make sure that you note this instruction carefully.

2) When you are ready to start work on the examination, that is as soon as the signal has been given, read the instructions to each question booklet, underline any key words or phrases, such as *least, best, outline, describe* and the like. In this way you will tend to answer as requested rather than discover on reviewing your paper that you *listed without describing*, that you selected the *worst* choice rather than the *best* choice, etc.

3) If the examination is of the objective or multiple-choice type – that is, each question will also give a series of possible answers: A, B, C or D, and you are called upon to select the best answer and write the letter next to that answer on your answer paper – it is advisable to start answering each question in turn. There may be anywhere from 50 to 100 such questions in the three or four hours allotted and you can see how much time would be taken if you read through all the questions before beginning to answer any. Furthermore, if you come across a question or group of questions which you know would be difficult to answer, it would undoubtedly affect your handling of all the other questions.

4) If the examination is of the essay type and contains but a few questions, it is a moot point as to whether you should read all the questions before starting to answer any one. Of course, if you are given a choice – say five out of seven and the like – then it is essential to read all the questions so you can eliminate the two that are most difficult. If, however, you are asked to answer all the questions, there may be danger in trying to answer the easiest one first because you may find that you will spend too much time on it. The best technique is to answer the first question, then proceed to the second, etc.

5) Time your answers. Before the exam begins, write down the time it started, then add the time allowed for the examination and write down the time it must be completed, then divide the time available somewhat as follows:
   - If 3-1/2 hours are allowed, that would be 210 minutes. If you have 80 objective-type questions, that would be an average of 2-1/2 minutes per question. Allow yourself no more than 2 minutes per question, or a total of 160 minutes, which will permit about 50 minutes to review.
   - If for the time allotment of 210 minutes there are 7 essay questions to answer, that would average about 30 minutes a question. Give yourself only 25 minutes per question so that you have about 35 minutes to review.

6) The most important instruction is to *read each question* and make sure you know what is wanted. The second most important instruction is to *time yourself properly* so that you answer every question. The third most important instruction is to *answer every question*. Guess if you have to but include something for each question. Remember that you will receive no credit for a blank and will probably receive some credit if you write something in answer to an essay question. If you guess a letter – say "B" for a multiple-choice question – you may have guessed right. If you leave a blank as an answer to a multiple-choice question, the examiners may respect your feelings but it will not add a point to your score. Some exams may penalize you for wrong answers, so in such cases *only*, you may not want to guess unless you have some basis for your answer.

7) Suggestions
   a. Objective-type questions
      1. Examine the question booklet for proper sequence of pages and questions
      2. Read all instructions carefully
      3. Skip any question which seems too difficult; return to it after all other questions have been answered
      4. Apportion your time properly; do not spend too much time on any single question or group of questions

5. Note and underline key words – *all, most, fewest, least, best, worst, same, opposite,* etc.
6. Pay particular attention to negatives
7. Note unusual option, e.g., unduly long, short, complex, different or similar in content to the body of the question
8. Observe the use of "hedging" words – *probably, may, most likely,* etc.
9. Make sure that your answer is put next to the same number as the question
10. Do not second-guess unless you have good reason to believe the second answer is definitely more correct
11. Cross out original answer if you decide another answer is more accurate; do not erase until you are ready to hand your paper in
12. Answer all questions; guess unless instructed otherwise
13. Leave time for review

b. Essay questions
1. Read each question carefully
2. Determine exactly what is wanted. Underline key words or phrases.
3. Decide on outline or paragraph answer
4. Include many different points and elements unless asked to develop any one or two points or elements
5. Show impartiality by giving pros and cons unless directed to select one side only
6. Make and write down any assumptions you find necessary to answer the questions
7. Watch your English, grammar, punctuation and choice of words
8. Time your answers; don't crowd material

8) Answering the essay question

Most essay questions can be answered by framing the specific response around several key words or ideas. Here are a few such key words or ideas:

M's: manpower, materials, methods, money, management
P's: purpose, program, policy, plan, procedure, practice, problems, pitfalls, personnel, public relations

a. Six basic steps in handling problems:
1. Preliminary plan and background development
2. Collect information, data and facts
3. Analyze and interpret information, data and facts
4. Analyze and develop solutions as well as make recommendations
5. Prepare report and sell recommendations
6. Install recommendations and follow up effectiveness

b. Pitfalls to avoid
1. *Taking things for granted* – A statement of the situation does not necessarily imply that each of the elements is necessarily true; for example, a complaint may be invalid and biased so that all that can be taken for granted is that a complaint has been registered

2. *Considering only one side of a situation* – Wherever possible, indicate several alternatives and then point out the reasons you selected the best one
3. *Failing to indicate follow up* – Whenever your answer indicates action on your part, make certain that you will take proper follow-up action to see how successful your recommendations, procedures or actions turn out to be
4. *Taking too long in answering any single question* – Remember to time your answers properly

IX. AFTER THE TEST

Scoring procedures differ in detail among civil service jurisdictions although the general principles are the same. Whether the papers are hand-scored or graded by machine we have described, they are nearly always graded by number. That is, the person who marks the paper knows only the number – never the name – of the applicant. Not until all the papers have been graded will they be matched with names. If other tests, such as training and experience or oral interview ratings have been given, scores will be combined. Different parts of the examination usually have different weights. For example, the written test might count 60 percent of the final grade, and a rating of training and experience 40 percent. In many jurisdictions, veterans will have a certain number of points added to their grades.

After the final grade has been determined, the names are placed in grade order and an eligible list is established. There are various methods for resolving ties between those who get the same final grade – probably the most common is to place first the name of the person whose application was received first. Job offers are made from the eligible list in the order the names appear on it. You will be notified of your grade and your rank as soon as all these computations have been made. This will be done as rapidly as possible.

People who are found to meet the requirements in the announcement are called "eligibles." Their names are put on a list of eligible candidates. An eligible's chances of getting a job depend on how high he stands on this list and how fast agencies are filling jobs from the list.

When a job is to be filled from a list of eligibles, the agency asks for the names of people on the list of eligibles for that job. When the civil service commission receives this request, it sends to the agency the names of the three people highest on this list. Or, if the job to be filled has specialized requirements, the office sends the agency the names of the top three persons who meet these requirements from the general list.

The appointing officer makes a choice from among the three people whose names were sent to him. If the selected person accepts the appointment, the names of the others are put back on the list to be considered for future openings.

That is the rule in hiring from all kinds of eligible lists, whether they are for typist, carpenter, chemist, or something else. For every vacancy, the appointing officer has his choice of any one of the top three eligibles on the list. This explains why the person whose name is on top of the list sometimes does not get an appointment when some of the persons lower on the list do. If the appointing officer chooses the second or third eligible, the No. 1 eligible does not get a job at once, but stays on the list until he is appointed or the list is terminated.

X. HOW TO PASS THE INTERVIEW TEST

The examination for which you applied requires an oral interview test. You have already taken the written test and you are now being called for the interview test – the final part of the formal examination.

You may think that it is not possible to prepare for an interview test and that there are no procedures to follow during an interview. Our purpose is to point out some things you can do in advance that will help you and some good rules to follow and pitfalls to avoid while you are being interviewed.

What is an interview supposed to test?

The written examination is designed to test the technical knowledge and competence of the candidate; the oral is designed to evaluate intangible qualities, not readily measured otherwise, and to establish a list showing the relative fitness of each candidate – as measured against his competitors – for the position sought. Scoring is not on the basis of "right" and "wrong," but on a sliding scale of values ranging from "not passable" to "outstanding." As a matter of fact, it is possible to achieve a relatively low score without a single "incorrect" answer because of evident weakness in the qualities being measured.

Occasionally, an examination may consist entirely of an oral test – either an individual or a group oral. In such cases, information is sought concerning the technical knowledges and abilities of the candidate, since there has been no written examination for this purpose. More commonly, however, an oral test is used to supplement a written examination.

Who conducts interviews?

The composition of oral boards varies among different jurisdictions. In nearly all, a representative of the personnel department serves as chairman. One of the members of the board may be a representative of the department in which the candidate would work. In some cases, "outside experts" are used, and, frequently, a businessman or some other representative of the general public is asked to serve. Labor and management or other special groups may be represented. The aim is to secure the services of experts in the appropriate field.

However the board is composed, it is a good idea (and not at all improper or unethical) to ascertain in advance of the interview who the members are and what groups they represent. When you are introduced to them, you will have some idea of their backgrounds and interests, and at least you will not stutter and stammer over their names.

What should be done before the interview?

While knowledge about the board members is useful and takes some of the surprise element out of the interview, there is other preparation which is more substantive. It *is* possible to prepare for an oral interview – in several ways:

1) Keep a copy of your application and review it carefully before the interview

This may be the only document before the oral board, and the starting point of the interview. Know what education and experience you have listed there, and the sequence and dates of all of it. Sometimes the board will ask you to review the highlights of your experience for them; you should not have to hem and haw doing it.

2) Study the class specification and the examination announcement

Usually, the oral board has one or both of these to guide them. The qualities, characteristics or knowledges required by the position sought are stated in these documents. They offer valuable clues as to the nature of the oral interview. For example, if the job involves supervisory responsibilities, the announcement will usually indicate that knowledge of modern supervisory methods and the qualifications of the candidate as a supervisor will be tested. If so, you can expect such questions, frequently in the form of a hypothetical situation which you are expected to solve. NEVER go into an oral without knowledge of the duties and responsibilities of the job you seek.

3) Think through each qualification required

Try to visualize the kind of questions you would ask if you were a board member. How well could you answer them? Try especially to appraise your own knowledge and background in each area, *measured against the job sought*, and identify any areas in which you are weak. Be critical and realistic – do not flatter yourself.

4) Do some general reading in areas in which you feel you may be weak

For example, if the job involves supervision and your past experience has NOT, some general reading in supervisory methods and practices, particularly in the field of human relations, might be useful. Do NOT study agency procedures or detailed manuals. The oral board will be testing your understanding and capacity, not your memory.

5) Get a good night's sleep and watch your general health and mental attitude

You will want a clear head at the interview. Take care of a cold or any other minor ailment, and of course, no hangovers.

What should be done on the day of the interview?

Now comes the day of the interview itself. Give yourself plenty of time to get there. Plan to arrive somewhat ahead of the scheduled time, particularly if your appointment is in the fore part of the day. If a previous candidate fails to appear, the board might be ready for you a bit early. By early afternoon an oral board is almost invariably behind schedule if there are many candidates, and you may have to wait. Take along a book or magazine to read, or your application to review, but leave any extraneous material in the waiting room when you go in for your interview. In any event, relax and compose yourself.

The matter of dress is important. The board is forming impressions about you – from your experience, your manners, your attitude, and your appearance. Give your personal appearance careful attention. Dress your best, but not your flashiest. Choose conservative, appropriate clothing, and be sure it is immaculate. This is a business interview, and your appearance should indicate that you regard it as such. Besides, being well groomed and properly dressed will help boost your confidence.

Sooner or later, someone will call your name and escort you into the interview room. *This is it.* From here on you are on your own. It is too late for any more preparation. But remember, you asked for this opportunity to prove your fitness, and you are here because your request was granted.

What happens when you go in?

The usual sequence of events will be as follows: The clerk (who is often the board stenographer) will introduce you to the chairman of the oral board, who will introduce you to the other members of the board. Acknowledge the introductions before you sit down. Do not be surprised if you find a microphone facing you or a stenotypist sitting by. Oral interviews are usually recorded in the event of an appeal or other review.

Usually the chairman of the board will open the interview by reviewing the highlights of your education and work experience from your application – primarily for the benefit of the other members of the board, as well as to get the material into the record. Do not interrupt or comment unless there is an error or significant misinterpretation; if that is the case, do not hesitate. But do not quibble about insignificant matters. Also, he will usually ask you some question about your education, experience or your present job – partly to get you to start talking and to establish the interviewing "rapport." He may start the actual questioning, or turn it over to one of the other members. Frequently, each member undertakes the questioning on a particular area, one in which he is perhaps most competent, so you can expect each member to participate in the examination. Because time is limited, you may also expect some rather abrupt switches in the direction the questioning takes, so do not be upset by it. Normally, a board member will not pursue a single line of questioning unless he discovers a particular strength or weakness.

After each member has participated, the chairman will usually ask whether any member has any further questions, then will ask you if you have anything you wish to add. Unless you are expecting this question, it may floor you. Worse, it may start you off on an extended, extemporaneous speech. The board is not usually seeking more information. The question is principally to offer you a last opportunity to present further qualifications or to indicate that you have nothing to add. So, if you feel that a significant qualification or characteristic has been overlooked, it is proper to point it out in a sentence or so. Do not compliment the board on the thoroughness of their examination – they have been sketchy, and you know it. If you wish, merely say, "No thank you, I have nothing further to add." This is a point where you can "talk yourself out" of a good impression or fail to present an important bit of information. Remember, *you close the interview yourself.*

The chairman will then say, "That is all, Mr. _____, thank you." Do not be startled; the interview is over, and quicker than you think. Thank him, gather your belongings and take your leave. Save your sigh of relief for the other side of the door.

How to put your best foot forward

Throughout this entire process, you may feel that the board individually and collectively is trying to pierce your defenses, seek out your hidden weaknesses and embarrass and confuse you. Actually, this is not true. They are obliged to make an appraisal of your qualifications for the job you are seeking, and they want to see you in your best light. Remember, they must interview all candidates and a non-cooperative candidate may become a failure in spite of their best efforts to bring out his qualifications. Here are 15 suggestions that will help you:

1) Be natural – Keep your attitude confident, not cocky

If you are not confident that you can do the job, do not expect the board to be. Do not apologize for your weaknesses, try to bring out your strong points. The board is interested in a positive, not negative, presentation. Cockiness will antagonize any board member and make him wonder if you are covering up a weakness by a false show of strength.

2) Get comfortable, but don't lounge or sprawl

Sit erectly but not stiffly. A careless posture may lead the board to conclude that you are careless in other things, or at least that you are not impressed by the importance of the occasion. Either conclusion is natural, even if incorrect. Do not fuss with your clothing, a pencil or an ashtray. Your hands may occasionally be useful to emphasize a point; do not let them become a point of distraction.

3) Do not wisecrack or make small talk

This is a serious situation, and your attitude should show that you consider it as such. Further, the time of the board is limited – they do not want to waste it, and neither should you.

4) Do not exaggerate your experience or abilities

In the first place, from information in the application or other interviews and sources, the board may know more about you than you think. Secondly, you probably will not get away with it. An experienced board is rather adept at spotting such a situation, so do not take the chance.

5) If you know a board member, do not make a point of it, yet do not hide it

Certainly you are not fooling him, and probably not the other members of the board. Do not try to take advantage of your acquaintanceship – it will probably do you little good.

6) Do not dominate the interview

Let the board do that. They will give you the clues – do not assume that you have to do all the talking. Realize that the board has a number of questions to ask you, and do not try to take up all the interview time by showing off your extensive knowledge of the answer to the first one.

7) Be attentive

You only have 20 minutes or so, and you should keep your attention at its sharpest throughout. When a member is addressing a problem or question to you, give him your undivided attention. Address your reply principally to him, but do not exclude the other board members.

8) Do not interrupt

A board member may be stating a problem for you to analyze. He will ask you a question when the time comes. Let him state the problem, and wait for the question.

9) Make sure you understand the question

Do not try to answer until you are sure what the question is. If it is not clear, restate it in your own words or ask the board member to clarify it for you. However, do not haggle about minor elements.

10) Reply promptly but not hastily

A common entry on oral board rating sheets is "candidate responded readily," or "candidate hesitated in replies." Respond as promptly and quickly as you can, but do not jump to a hasty, ill-considered answer.

11) Do not be peremptory in your answers

A brief answer is proper – but do not fire your answer back. That is a losing game from your point of view. The board member can probably ask questions much faster than you can answer them.

12) Do not try to create the answer you think the board member wants

He is interested in what kind of mind you have and how it works – not in playing games. Furthermore, he can usually spot this practice and will actually grade you down on it.

13) Do not switch sides in your reply merely to agree with a board member

Frequently, a member will take a contrary position merely to draw you out and to see if you are willing and able to defend your point of view. Do not start a debate, yet do not surrender a good position. If a position is worth taking, it is worth defending.

14) Do not be afraid to admit an error in judgment if you are shown to be wrong
   The board knows that you are forced to reply without any opportunity for careful consideration. Your answer may be demonstrably wrong. If so, admit it and get on with the interview.

15) Do not dwell at length on your present job
   The opening question may relate to your present assignment. Answer the question but do not go into an extended discussion. You are being examined for a *new* job, not your present one. As a matter of fact, try to phrase ALL your answers in terms of the job for which you are being examined.

Basis of Rating
   Probably you will forget most of these "do's" and "don'ts" when you walk into the oral interview room. Even remembering them all will not ensure you a passing grade. Perhaps you did not have the qualifications in the first place. But remembering them will help you to put your best foot forward, without treading on the toes of the board members.
   Rumor and popular opinion to the contrary notwithstanding, an oral board wants you to make the best appearance possible. They know you are under pressure – but they also want to see how you respond to it as a guide to what your reaction would be under the pressures of the job you seek. They will be influenced by the degree of poise you display, the personal traits you show and the manner in which you respond.

ABOUT THIS BOOK

   This book contains tests divided into Examination Sections. Go through each test, answering every question in the margin. We have also attached a sample answer sheet at the back of the book that can be removed and used. At the end of each test look at the answer key and check your answers. On the ones you got wrong, look at the right answer choice and learn. Do not fill in the answers first. Do not memorize the questions and answers, but understand the answer and principles involved. On your test, the questions will likely be different from the samples. Questions are changed and new ones added. If you understand these past questions you should have success with any changes that arise. Tests may consist of several types of questions. We have additional books on each subject should more study be advisable or necessary for you. Finally, the more you study, the better prepared you will be. This book is intended to be the last thing you study before you walk into the examination room. Prior study of relevant texts is also recommended. NLC publishes some of these in our Fundamental Series. Knowledge and good sense are important factors in passing your exam. Good luck also helps. So now study this Passbook, absorb the material contained within and take that knowledge into the examination. Then do your best to pass that exam.

EXAMINATION SECTION

EXAMINATION SECTION
TEST 1

DIRECTIONS: Each question or incomplete statement is followed by several suggested answers or completions. Select the one that BEST answers the question or completes the statement. *PRINT THE LETTER OF THE CORRECT ANSWER IN THE SPACE AT THE RIGHT.*

1. A specialist is meeting with a panel of local community leaders to determine their perceptions about the effectiveness of a recent outreach program. The leaders seem unresponsive to the specialist's questions, looking at the floor or each other without directly answering the specialist's questions. One strategy that might work to elicit the desired information would be to

    A. try to discern the hidden meaning of their silence
    B. adopt a mildly confrontational tone and remind them of what's at stake in the community
    C. keep asking open-ended questions and wait patiently for responses
    D. tell them to come back when they're ready to tell you their opinions

1.____

2. Each of the following statements about maintaining a community's attention is true, EXCEPT

    A. The more challenging it is to pay attention to a message, the more likely it is that it will be attended to.
    B. Listeners will be more motivated to pay attention if a speech is personally meaningful.
    C. People will be more likely to attend if a speaker pauses to suggest natural transitions in a speech.
    D. Listeners will attend to messages that stand out.

2.____

3. Each of the following is a key strategy to integrative bargaining among community members in conflict, EXCEPT

    A. focusing on positions, rather than interests
    B. separating the people from the problem
    C. aiming for an outcome based on an objectively identified standard
    D. using active listening skills, such as rephrasing and questioning

3.____

4. Which of the following is NOT one of the major variables to take into account when considering a community needs assessment?

    A. State of program development
    B. Resources available
    C. Demographics
    D. Community attitudes

4.____

5. Which of the following groups would probably be formed specifically for, or be involved in, the purpose of addressing a specific unmet community need?

    A. An existing consumer group
    B. A council of community representatives
    C. A committee
    D. An existing community organization

5.____

6. If a public outreach campaign designed to mobilize a community fails, the most likely reason for this failure is that the campaign

   A. was not specific about what they want people to do
   B. are overly serious and do not appeal to people's sense of humor
   C. offered no incentive for the audience to make a change
   D. did not use language that appealed to the audience's emotions

7. Nationwide, the rate of involvement of elderly people in community-based programs demonstrates that they are

   A. underserved when compared to other age groups
   B. served at about the same rate as other age groups
   C. over-served when compared to other age groups
   D. hardly served at all

8. In projecting the likelihood of an education program's success, a domestic violence specialist identifies every single event that must occur to complete the project. The specialist then arranges these events in sequential order and allocates time requirements for each. Finally, the total time is calculated and a model showing all their events and timelines is charted. The specialist has used

   A. a PERT chart
   B. a simulation
   C. a Markov model
   D. the critical path method

9. When working with members of a predominantly African-American community, specialists from other cultural backgrounds should be aware that African Americans tend to express thoughts and feelings through descriptions of

   A. physically tangible sensations
   B. problems to be analyzed
   C. corresponding analogies
   D. spiritual issues

10. Local nonprofessionals should be considered useful to a specialist who is looking to undertake a community outreach or educational initiative. Which of the following is LEAST likely to be a characteristic or role demonstrated by these community members?

    A. Undertaking support functions at the agency
    B. Serving as a communication channel between the agency and clients
    C. Encouraging greater agency acceptance and credibility within the community
    D. Helping the agency to accomplish meaningful change

11. In working with Native American groups or clients, it is important to recognize that the greatest health problem facing their communities today is

    A. domestic violence
    B. depression and suicide
    C. alcoholism
    D. tuberculosis

12. A specialist is facilitating a cooperative conflict resolution session between community members who have different opinions about what kinds of intervention services should be offered by the local adult protective services agency. Which of the following is NOT a guideline that should be followed in this process?

    A. Early in the negotiations, ask each party to name the issues on which they will positively not yield.
    B. Try to get the parties to view the issue from other points of view, beside the two or three conflicting ones.
    C. Have each side volunteer what it would be willing to do to resolve the conflict.
    D. At the end of the session, draw up a formal agreement with agreed-upon actions for both parties.

13. A specialist wants to evaluate the effectiveness of a local women's shelter. The shelter has suffered from lax participation, given the number of women who have been abused in the surrounding area. The specialist wants to speak with the women in the community who did not follow up on referrals to the shelter, and begins by visiting some of these women. After gaining the trust of these women, the specialist asks for the names of women they know who might be in need of help with a domestic violence situation. The specialist's approach in this case is _____ sampling.

    A. maximum variation   B. snowball
    C. convenience   D. typical case

14. When it comes to perceiving messages, people typically DON'T

    A. tend to simplify causal connections and sometimes even seek a single cause to explain what may be a highly complex effect
    B. tend to perceive messages independently of a categorical framework, especially if the message may be distorted by such an interpretation
    C. have a predisposition toward accepting any pattern that a speaker offers to explain seemingly unconnected facts
    D. tend to interpret things in the way they are viewed by their reference group

15. The elder members of Native American communities, regardless of kinship, are most commonly referred to as

    A. the ancients   B. father or mother
    C. grandfather or grandmother   D. chiefs

16. Each of the following is typically an objective of community mobilization, EXCEPT

    A. To convince existing community resources to alter their services or work together to address an unmet need
    B. To gather and distribute information to consumers and agencies about unmet needs
    C. To publicize existing community resources and make them more accessible
    D. To bring an unmet community need to public attention in order to achieve acceptance of and support for fulfilling the need

17. Research in community outreach shows that women often build friendships through shared positive feelings, whereas men often build friendships through

    A. metacommunication
    B. catharsis
    C. impression management
    D. shared activities

18. Typically, the FIRST step in a community needs assessment is to

    A. identify community's strengths
    B. explore the nature of the neighborhood
    C. get to know the area and its residents
    D. talk to people in the community

19. Most public relations experts agree that _____ exposure(s) to a message is the minimum just to get the message noticed. If the aim of a public outreach campaign is action or a change in behavior, the agency budget must plan for more exposures.

    A. one   B. two   C. three   D. four

20. In the program development/community liaison model of community work and public outreach, the primary constituency is considered to be

    A. community representatives and the service agency board or administrators
    B. elected officials, social agencies, and interagency organizations
    C. marginalized or oppressed population groups in a city or region
    D. residents of a neighborhood, parish or rural county

21. Social or interpersonal problems in many African American communities have their roots in

    A. personality deficits
    B. unresolved family conflicts
    C. poor communication
    D. external stressors

22. A public outreach campaign should
    I. focus on short-term, measurable goals, rather than ultimate outcomes
    II. try to alter entrenched attitudes within a short time, with powerfully worded messages
    III. proceed in steps or phases, each of which lays out a mechanism that leads to the desired effect
    IV. ignore causes that led to a problem, and instead focus on solutions

    A. I and II   B. II and III   C. III only   D. I, II, III and IV

23. Research findings indicate that in listing preferences for helping professional attributes, individuals from culturally diverse groups are MOST likely to _____ as more important than

    A. personality similarity; either race/ethnic similarity or attitude similarity
    B. therapist experience; any kind of similarity
    C. race/ethnic similarity; attitude similarity
    D. attitude similarity; race/ethnic similarity

24. Each of the following is considered to be an objective of community organization, EXCEPT

    A. effecting changes in the distribution of decision-making power
    B. helping people develop and strengthen the traits of self-direction and cooperation
    C. effecting and maintaining the balance between needs and resources in a community
    D. helping people deal with their problems by developing alternative behaviors

25. A specialist is helping the adult protective services agency to design a public outreach campaign. The topic to be addressed is complex, public understanding is low, and most professionals at the agency feel that having more complete information might change the opinions of community members. Which method of pre-campaign research is probably most appropriate?

    A. Deliberative polling
    B. Attitude scales
    C. Surveys or questionnaires
    D. Focus groups

KEY (CORRECT ANSWERS)

1. C	11. C
2. A	12. A
3. A	13. B
4. C	14. B
5. C	15. C
6. A	16. B
7. A	17. D
8. D	18. B
9. C	19. C
10. A	20. A

21. D
22. C
23. D
24. D
25. A

TEST 2

DIRECTIONS: Each question or incomplete statement is followed by several suggested answers or completions. Select the one the BEST answers the question or completes the statement. *PRINT THE LETTER OF THE CORRECT ANSWER IN THE SPACE AT THE RIGHT.*

1. A specialist has been called in to resolve a dispute between two community leaders who have been arguing about the level of service needed within the community. The discussion has been going on for several hours when the specialist arrives, and both people seem to be upset. After calming the two down and getting each of them to agree on a statement of the problem, the specialist should ask each person to   1._____

    A. summarize his or her argument in three main points
    B. explain why he or she became so upset
    C. clearly state, in objective terms, the position of the other in a form that meets with the other's approval
    D. identify the best alternative outcome, other than their presumed ideal

2. In evaluation the impact of a public outreach campaign, the _____ model can be used early in he campaign to address first impressions.   2._____

    A. exposure or advertising
    B. expert interview
    C. impact monitoring or process
    D. experimental or quasi-experimental

3. When trying to motivate an older population to take action on a community problem, it is helpful to remember that older people   3._____

    A. are more self-reliant in their decision-making than other members of the same family
    B. often need more time to decide than younger people
    C. are more likely than younger people to view community problems self-referentially
    D. tend to take a pragmatic, rather than philosophical, view of life

4. The method of group or community decision-making that is normally most time-consuming is   4._____

    A. majority opinion
    B. consensus
    C. expert opinion
    D. authority rule

5. A local adult protective services agency has identified one of the goals of its recent public outreach campaign to be the mobilization of activists. The campaign should probably   5._____

    A. target neutral audiences
    B. home in on supporters
    C. stick to purely factual information
    D. try to persuade community fence-sitters

6. Research of Native American youths' perceptions of family concerns for their well-being has generally found that these youths

   A. have a high degree of uncertainty about their families' feelings toward them
   B. believe their families don't care about them
   C. believe that their mothers care a great deal about them, but their fathers don't
   D. believe their families care a great deal about them

7. A domestic violence specialist is developing a new outreach program for the local community. The specialist has defined the target problem, set program goals, and planned the actions that will take place as a result of the program. Most likely, the next step will be to

   A. evaluate the resources available to achieve program goals
   B. define and sequence the steps that will be taken to achieve program goals
   C. determine how the program will be evaluated
   D. decide how the program will operate

8. In the following exchange, what listening skill is evident in the underlined statement?

   Elder: I'm so glad to have someone to talk to, someone who really understands my problem.
   Specialist: <u>It is nice to be able to talk to someone who will listen.</u>
   Elder: That's for sure.

   A. verbatim response
   B. paraphrasing
   C. advising
   D. evaluation

9. Which of the following activities is involved in the specialist's task of mobilizing?

   A. Meeting individuals in the community with problems and assisting them in finding help
   B. Identifying unmet community needs
   C. Speaking out against an unjust policy or procedure
   D. Developing new services or linking presently available services to meet community needs

10. The preliminary research associated with a public outreach campaign should FIRST be aimed at determining

    A. the budget
    B. the message's ultimate audience
    C. what media to use
    D. the short-term behavioral goals of the campaign

11. A specialist in a low-income community wants to plan programs that will deal with the influence of unemployment on domestic disturbances. The specialist needs to know not only how many unemployed people are in the community now, but also how many people will be unemployed at any particular time in the future, and how those numbers will vary given certain conditions. Probably the best way to trace employment rates over time and within differing conditions is through the use of

A. the critical path method B. linear programming
C. difference equations D. the Markov model

12. Generally, public outreach programs—whatever their stated goal—should
    I. create a sense of urgency about a problem
    II. decline to identify opponents of the issue or idea
    III. propose concrete, easily understandable solutions
    IV. urge a specific action

    A. I only   B. I, III and IV   C. II and III   D. I, II, III and IV

13. Which of the following methods of community needs assessment relies to the greatest degree on existing public records?

    A. Social indicators B. Field study
    C. Rates-under treatment D. Key informant

14. During an interview with a Native American client, a specialist is careful to maintain close and nearly constant eye contact. The client is most likely to interpret this as

    A. a show of high concern
    B. a sign of disrespect
    C. an uncomfortable assumption of intimacy
    D. an attempt to intimidate

15. The best strategy for addressing an audience that is known to be captive, or even hostile, is to

    A. refer to experiences in common
    B. flatter the audience
    C. joke about things in or near the audience
    D. plead for fairness

16. Integrative conflict resolution is characterized by

    A. an overriding concern to maximize joint outcomes
    B. one side's interests opposing the other's
    C. a fixed and limited amount of resources to be divided, so that the more one group gets, the less another gets
    D. manipulation and withholding information as negotiation strategies

17. A specialist wants to learn how to interact with the members of a largely Latino community in a more culturally sensitive way. Which of the following is NOT a guideline for interacting with members of a Latino community?

    A. Efforts to foster independence and self-reliance may be interpreted by many Latinos as a lack of concern for others.
    B. Efforts to deal one-on-one with an adolescent client may serve to alienate the parents, especially the mother.
    C. A nonverbal gesture such as lowering the eyes is interpreted by many Latinos as a sign of respect and deference to authority.
    D. In much of Latino culture, the locus of control for problems tends to be much more external than internal.

18. Each of the following is an supporting assumption of community organization, EXCEPT   18._____

    A. democracy requires cooperative participation
    B. in order for communities to change, it is necessary for each individual in the community to be willing to change
    C. communities often need help with organization and planning
    D. holistic approaches work better than fragmented or ad-hoc programs

19. Helping professionals often have difficulty to bring community resources together to fulfill unmet community needs. Which of the following is NOT usually a reason for this?   19._____

    A. Some community groups resist assistance when it is offered.
    B. Few community groups make their needs known.
    C. Community resources frequently change the type of services they offer.
    D. Often, community resources prefer to work alone

20. When dealing with groups or populations of elderly clients, specialists should be mindful that about _____ of the nation's elderly suffer from mental health problems.   20._____

    A. a tenth   B. a quarter   C. a third   D. half

21. In an African American community, a specialist from another culture should recognize that church participation, for most African Americans, is viewed as a   21._____

    A. method for maintaining control and communicating competency
    B. way of depersonalizing problems or troubles
    C. way to divert attention away from problems
    D. means of cathartic emotional release

22. Adult protective service programs supported by state statutes protect elderly people from abuse and neglect under the doctrine of   22._____

    A. parens patriae   B. habeas corpus
    C. in loco parentis   D. volenti non fit injuria

23. In terms of public outreach, which of the following statements about an audience is NOT generally true?   23._____

    A. The more heterogeneous the audience, the more necessary it will be to use specific examples and appeals to certain types of people
    B. The smaller the audience, the more likely that its members will share assumptions and values
    C. When the speaker does not know the status of an audience, it is best to assume that they are captive rather than voluntary
    D. The larger an audience, the more formal a presentation is likely to be

24. A specialist often spends time in the places frequented by community residents. She listens carefully to what residents seem most concerned about, and engages many in conversations, asking them how they see the problems in the community. During these conversations, she makes mental notes about whether the statements of the problems are the same things that are mentioned in their conversations. From these conversations, the worker determines what she thinks the unmet needs of the community are. Which of the key issues in identifying unmet needs has the worker neglected to address?

    A. The different points of view regarding the issues, and whether there is any common ground.
    B. Whether the stated problems and the conversations with community residents reflect the same concerns.
    C. How community residents define the issues.
    D. What the residents talk about with one another in a community.

25. Which of the following political styles should be used to promote an issue that could become controversial if it is perceived to involve major reforms?

    A. High-conflict, polarized
    B. High-conflict, consensual
    C. Moderate conflict, compromise-oriented
    D. Low-conflict, technical

KEY (CORRECT ANSWERS)

1.	C	11.	D
2.	A	12.	B
3.	B	13.	A
4.	B	14.	B
5.	B	15.	A
6.	D	16.	A
7.	A	17.	D
8.	B	18.	B
9.	D	19.	C
10.	B	20.	B

21. D
22. A
23. A
24. A
25. D

EXAMINATION SECTION
TEST 1

DIRECTIONS: Each question or incomplete statement is followed by several suggested answers or completions. Select the one that BEST answers the question or completes the statement. *PRINT THE LETTER OF THE CORRECT ANSWER IN THE SPACE AT THE RIGHT.*

1. When conducting a needs assessment for the purpose of education planning, an agency's FIRST step is to identify or provide

   A. a profile of population characteristics
   B. barriers to participation
   C. existing resources
   D. profiles of competing resources

   1._____

2. Research has demonstrated that of the following, the most effective medium for communicating with external publics is/are

   A. video news releases
   B. television
   C. radio
   D. newspapers

   2._____

3. Basic ideas behind the effort to influence the attitudes and behaviors of a constituency include each of the following, EXCEPT the idea that

   A. words, rather than actions or events, are most likely to motivate
   B. demands for action are a usual response
   C. self-interest usually figures heavily into public involvement
   D. the reliability of change programs is difficult to assess

   3._____

4. An agency representative is trying to craft a pithy message to constituents in order to encourage the use agency program resources. Choosing an audience for such messages is easiest when the message

   A. is project- or behavior-based
   B. is combined with other messages
   C. is abstract
   D. has a broad appeal

   4._____

5. Of the following factors, the most important to the success of an agency's external education or communication programs is the

   A. amount of resources used to implement them
   B. public's prior experiences with the agency
   C. real value of the program to the public
   D. commitment of the internal audience

   5._____

6. A representative for a state agency is being interviewed by a reporter from a local news network. The representative is being asked to defend a program that is extremely unpopular in certain parts of the municipality. When a constituency is known to be opposed to a position, the most useful communication strategy is to present

   6._____

A. only the arguments that are consistent with constituents' views
B. only the agency's side of the issue
C. both sides of the argument as clearly as possible
D. both sides of the argument, omitting key information about the opposing position

7. The most significant barriers to effective agency community relations include
   I. widespread distrust of communication strategies
   II. the media's "watchdog" stance
   III. public apathy
   IV. statutory opposition

   A. I only
   B. I and II
   C. II and III
   D. III and IV

8. In conducting an education program, many agencies use workshops and seminars in a classroom setting. Advantages of classroom-style teaching over other means of educating the public include each of the following, EXCEPT:

   A. enabling an instructor to verify learning through testing and interaction with the target audience
   B. enabling hands-on practice and other participatory learning techniques
   C. ability to reach an unlimited number of participants in a given length of time
   D. ability to convey the latest, most up-to-date information

9. The _____ model of community relations is characterized by an attempt to persuade the public to adopt the agency's point of view.

   A. two-way symmetric
   B. two-way asymmetric
   C. public information
   D. press agency/publicity

10. Important elements of an internal situation analysis include the
    I. list of agency opponents
    II. communication audit
    III. updated organizational almanac
    IV. stakeholder analysis

    A. I and II
    B. I, II and III
    C. II and III
    D. I, II, III and IV

11. Government agency information efforts typically involve each of the following objectives, EXCEPT to

    A. implement changes in the policies of government agencies to align with public opinion
    B. communicate the work of agencies
    C. explain agency techniques in a way that invites input from citizens
    D. provide citizen feedback to government administrators

12. Factors that are likely to influence the effectiveness of an educational campaign include the

    I. level of homogeneity among intended participants
    II. number and types of media used
    III. receptivity of the intended participants
    IV. level of specificity in the message or behavior to be taught

    A. I and II
    B. I, II and III
    C. II and III
    D. I, II, III and IV

13. An agency representative is writing instructional objectives that will later help to measure the effectiveness of an educational program. Which of the following verbs, included in an objective, would be MOST helpful for the purpose of measuring effectiveness?

    A. Know
    B. Identify
    C. Learn
    D. Comprehend

14. A state education agency wants to encourage participation in a program that has just received a boost through new federal legislation. The program is intended to include participants from a wide variety of socioeconomic and other demographic characteristics. The agency wants to launch a broad-based program that will inform virtually every interested party in the state about the program's new circumstances. In attempting to deliver this message to such a wide-ranging constituency, the agency's best practice would be to

    A. broadcast the same message through as many different media channels as possible
    B. focus on one discrete segment of the public at a time
    C. craft a message whose appeal is as broad as the public itself
    D. let the program's achievements speak for themselves and rely on word-of-mouth

15. Advantages associated with using the World Wide Web as an educational tool include

    I. an appeal to younger generations of the public
    II. visually-oriented, interactive learning
    III. learning that is not confined by space, time, or institutional as sociation
    IV. a variety of methods for verifying use and learning

    A. I only
    B. I and II
    C. I, II and III
    D. I, II, III and IV

16. In agencies involved in health care, community relations is a critical function because it

    A. serves as an intermediary between the agency and consumers
    B. generates a clear mission statement for agency goals and priorities
    C. ensures patient privacy while satisfying the media's right to information
    D. helps marketing professionals determine the wants and needs of agency constituents

17. After an extensive campaign to promote its newest program to constituents, an agency 17.____
    learns that most of the audience did not understand the intended message. Most likely,
    the agency has

    A. chosen words that were intended to inform, rather than persuade
    B. not accurately interpreted what the audience really needed to know
    C. overestimated the ability of the audience to receive and process the message
    D. compensated for noise that may have interrupted the message

18. The necessary elements that lead to conviction and motivation in the minds of partici- 18.____
    pants in an educational or information program include each of the following, EXCEPT
    the _____ of the message.

    A. acceptability
    B. intensity
    C. single-channel appeal
    D. pervasiveness

19. Printed materials are often at the core of educational programs provided by public agen- 19.____
    cies. The primary disadvantage associated with print is that it

    A. does not enable comprehensive treatment of a topic
    B. is generally unreliable in term of assessing results
    C. is often the most expensive medium available
    D. is constrained by time

20. Traditional thinking on public opinion holds that there is about _____ percent of the pub- 20.____
    lic who are pivotal to shifting the balance and momentum of opinion—they are concerned
    about an issue, but not fanatical, and interested enough to pay attention to a reasoned
    discussion.

    A. 2
    B. 10
    C. 33
    D. 51

21. One of the most useful guidelines for influencing attitude change among people is to 21.____

    A. inviting the target audience to come to you, rather than approaching them
    B. use moral appeals as the primary approach
    C. use concrete images to enable people to see the results of behaviors or indiffer-
       ence
    D. offer tangible rewards to people for changes in behaviors

22. An agency is attempting to evaluate the effectiveness of its educational program. For this 22.____
    purpose, it wants to observe several focus groups discussing the same program. Which
    of the following would NOT be a guideline for the use of focus groups?

    A. Focus groups should only include those who have participated in the program.
    B. Be sure to accurately record the discussion.
    C. The same questions should be asked at each focus group meeting.
    D. It is often helpful to have a neutral, non-agency employee facilitate discussions.

23. Research consistently shows that _____ is the determinant most likely to make a newspaper editor run a news release. 23._____

    A. novelty
    B. prominence
    C. proximity
    D. conflict

24. Which of the following is NOT one of the major variables to take into account when considering a population needs assessment? 24._____

    A. State of program development
    B. Resources available
    C. Demographics
    D. Community attitudes

25. The first step in any communications audit is to 25._____

    A. develop a research instrument
    B. determine how the organization currently communicates
    C. hire a contractor
    D. determine which audience to assess

KEY (CORRECT ANSWERS)

1. A
2. D
3. A
4. A
5. D

6. C
7. D
8. C
9. B
10. C

11. A
12. D
13. B
14. B
15. C

16. A
17. B
18. C
19. B
20. B

21. C
22. A
23. C
24. C
25. D

TEST 2

DIRECTIONS: Each question or incomplete statement is followed by several suggested answers or completions. Select the one that BEST answers the question or completes the statement. *PRINT THE LETTER OF THE CORRECT ANSWER IN THE SPACE AT THE RIGHT.*

1. A public relations practitioner at an agency has just composed a press release highlighting a program's recent accomplishments and success stories. In pitching such releases to print outlets, the practitioner should
    I. e-mail, mail, or send them by messenger
    II. address them to "editor" or "news director"
    III. have an assistant call all media contacts by telephone
    IV. ask reporters or editors how they prefer to receive them

    A. I and II   B. I and IV   C. II, III and IV   D. III only

2. The "output goals" of an educational program are MOST likely to include

    A. specified ratings of services by participants on a standardized scale
    B. observable effects on a given community or clientele
    C. the number of instructional hours provided
    D. the number of participants served

3. An agency wants to evaluate satisfaction levels among program participants, and mails out questionnaires to everyone who has been enrolled in the last year. The primary problem associated with this method of evaluative research is that it

    A. poses a significant inconvenience for respondents
    B. is inordinately expensive
    C. does not allow for follow-up or clarification questions
    D. usually involves a low response rate

4. A communications audit is an important tool for measuring

    A. the depth of penetration of a particular message or program
    B. the cost of the organization's information campaigns
    C. how key audiences perceive an organization
    D. the commitment of internal stakeholders

5. The "ABC's" of written learning objectives include each of the following, EXCEPT

    A. Audience   B. Behavior   C. Conditions   D. Delineation

6. When attempting to change the behaviors of constituents, it is important to keep in mind that
    I. most people are skeptical of communications that try to get them to change their behaviors
    II. in most cases, a person selects the media to which he exposes himself
    III. people tend to react defensively to messages or programs that rely on fear as a motivating factor
    IV. programs should aim for the broadest appeal possible in order to include as many participants as possible

    A. I and II   B. I, II and III   C. II and III   D. I, II, III and IV

7. The "laws" of public opinion include the idea that it is

   A. useful for anticipating emergencies
   B. not sensitive to important events
   C. basically determined by self-interest
   D. sustainable through persistent appeals

8. Which of the following types of evaluations is used to measure public attitudes before and after an information/educational program?

   A. retrieval study
   B. copy test
   C. quota sampling
   D. benchmark study

9. The primary source for internal communications is/are usually

   A. flow charts
   B. meetings
   C. voice mail
   D. printed publications

10. An agency representative is putting together informational materials brochures and a newsletter outlining changes in one of the state's biggest benefits programs. In assembling print materials as a medium for delivering information to the public, the representative should keep in mind each of the following trends:
    I. For various reasons, the reading capabilities of the public are in general decline
    II. Without tables and graphs to help illustrate the changes, it is unlikely that the message will be delivered effectively
    III. Professionals and career-oriented people are highly receptive to information written in the form of a journal article or empirical study
    IV. People tend to be put off by print materials that use itemized and bulleted (•) lists.

    A. I and II   B. I, II and III   C. II and III   D. I, II, III and IV

11. Which of the following steps in a problem-oriented information campaign would typically be implemented FIRST?

    A. Deciding on tactics
    B. Determining a communications strategy
    C. Evaluating the problem's impact
    D. Developing an organizational strategy

12. A common pitfall in conducting an educational program is to 12._____

    A. aim it at the wrong target audience
    B. overfund it
    C. leave it in the hands of people who are in the business of education, rather than those with expertise in the business of the organization
    D. ignore the possibility that some other organization is meeting the same educational need for the target audience

13. The key factors that affect the credibility of an agency's educational program include 13._____

    A. organization
    B. scope
    C. sophistication
    D. penetration

14. Research on public opinion consistently demonstrates that it is 14._____

    A. easy to move people toward a strong opinion on anything, as long as they are approached directly through their emotions
    B. easier to move people away from an opinion they currently hold than to have them form an opinion about something they have not previously cared about
    C. easy to move people toward a strong opinion on anything, as long as the message appeals to their reason and intellect
    D. difficult to move people toward a strong opinion on anything, no matter what the approach

15. In conducting an education program, many agencies use meetings and conferences to educate an audience about the organization and its programs. Advantages associated with this approach include 15._____
    I. a captive audience that is known to be interested in the topic
    II. ample opportunities for verifying learning
    III. cost-efficient meeting space
    IV. the ability to provide information on a wider variety of subjects

    A. I and II
    B. I, III and IV
    C. II and III
    D. I, II, III and IV

16. An agency is attempting to evaluate the effectiveness of its educational programs. For this purpose, it wants to observe several focus groups discussing particular programs. For this purpose, a focus group should never number more than _____ participants. 16._____

    A. 5   B. 10   C. 15   D. 20

17. A _____ speech is written so that several agency members can deliver it to different audiences with only minor variations. 17._____

    A. basic   B. printed   C. quota   D. pattern

18. Which of the following statements about public opinion is generally considered to be FALSE?   18._____

    A. Opinion is primarily reactive rather than proactive.
    B. People have more opinions about goals than about the means by which to achieve them.
    C. Facts tend to shift opinion in the accepted direction when opinion is not solidly structured.
    D. Public opinion is based more on information than desire.

19. An agency is trying to promote its educational program. As a general rule, the agency should NOT assume that   19._____

    A. people will only participate if they perceive an individual benefit
    B. promotions need to be aimed at small, discrete groups
    C. if the program is good, the audience will find out about it
    D. a variety of methods, including advertising, special events, and direct mail, should be considered

20. In planning a successful educational program, probably the first and most important question for an agency to ask is: 20._____

    A. What will be the content of the program?
    B. Who will be served by the program?
    C. When is the best time to schedule the program?
    D. Why is the program necessary?

21. Media kits are LEAST likely to contain   21._____

    A. fact sheets
    B. memoranda
    C. photographs with captions
    D. news releases

22. The use of pamphlets and booklets as media for communication with the public often involves the disadvantage that   22._____

    A. the messages contained within them are frequently nonspecific
    B. it is difficult to measure their effectiveness in delivering the message
    C. there are few opportunities for people to refer to them
    D. color reproduction is poor

23. The most important prerequisite of a good educational program is an   23._____

    A. abundance of resources to implement it
    B. individual staff unit formed for the purpose of program delivery
    C. accurate needs assessment
    D. uneducated constituency

24. After an education program has been delivered, an agency conducts a program evaluation to determine whether its objectives have been met. General rules about how to conduct such an education program evaluation include each of the following, EXCEPT that it

 A. must be done immediately after the program has been implemented
 B. should be simple and easy to use
 C. should be designed so that tabulation of responses can take place quickly and inexpensively
 D. should solicit mostly subjective, open-ended responses if the audience was large

25. Using electronic media such as television as means of educating the public is typically recommended ONLY for agencies that
 I. have a fairly simple message to begin with
 II. want to reach the masses, rather than a targeted audience
 III. have substantial financial resources
 IV. accept that they will not be able to measure the results of the campaign with much precision

 A. I and II
 B. I, II and III
 C. II and IV
 D. I, II, III and IV

KEY (CORRECT ANSWERS)

1. B	11. C
2. C	12. D
3. D	13. A
4. C	14. D
5. D	15. B
6. B	16. B
7. C	17. D
8. D	18. D
9. D	19. C
10. A	20. D

21. B
22. B
23. C
24. D
25. D

EXAMINATION SECTION
TEST 1

DIRECTIONS: Each question or incomplete statement is followed by several suggested answers or completions. Select the one that BEST answers the question or completes the statement. *PRINT THE LETTER OF THE CORRECT ANSWER IN THE SPACE AT THE RIGHT.*

1. Good procedure in handling complaints from the public may be divided into the following four principal stages:
    I. Investigation of the complaint
    II. Receipt of the complaint
    III. Assignment of responsibility for investigation and correction
    IV. Notification of correction
   The ORDER in which these stages ordinarily come is:

   A. III, II, I, IV
   B. II, III, I, IV
   C. II, III, IV, I
   D. II, IV, III, I

   1._____

2. The department may expect the MOST severe public criticism if

   A. it asks for an increase in its annual budget
   B. it purchases new and costly street cleaning equipment
   C. sanitation officers and men are reclassified to higher salary grades
   D. there is delay in cleaning streets of snow

   2._____

3. The MOST important function of public relations in the department should be to

   A. develop cooperation on the part of the public in keeping streets clean
   B. get stricter penalties enacted for health code violations
   C. recruit candidates for entrance positions who can be developed into supervisors
   D. train career personnel so that they can advance in the department

   3._____

4. The one of the following which has MOST frequently elicited unfavorable public comment has been

   A. dirty sidewalks or streets
   B. dumping on lots
   C. failure to curb dogs
   D. overflowing garbage cans

   4._____

5. It has been suggested that, as a public relations measure, sections hold *open house* for the public.
   The MOST effective time for this would be

   A. during the summer when children are not in school and can accompany their parents
   B. during the winter when snow is likely to fall and the public can see snow removal preparations
   C. immediately after a heavy snow storm when department snow removal operations are in full progress
   D. when street sanitation is receiving general attention as during *Keep City Clean* week

   5._____

6. When a public agency conducts a public relations program, it is MOST likely to find that each recipient of its message will

   A. disagree with the basic purpose of the message if the officials are not well known to him
   B. accept the message if it is presented by someone perceived as having a definite intention to persuade
   C. ignore the message unless it is presented in a literate and clever manner
   D. give greater attention to certain portions of the message as a result of his individual and cultural differences

7. Following are three statements about public relations and communications:
   I. A person who seeks to influence public opinion can speed up a trend
   II. Mass communications is the exposure of a mass audience to an idea
   III. All media are equally effective in reaching opinion leaders

   Which of the following choices CORRECTLY classifies the above statements into those which are correct and those which are not?

   A. I and II are correct, but III is not
   B. II and III are correct, but I is not
   C. I and III are correct, but II is not
   D. III is correct, but I and II are not

8. Public relations experts say that MAXIMUM effect for a message results from

   A. concentrating in one medium
   B. ignoring mass media and concentrating on *opinion makers*
   C. presenting only those factors which support a given position
   D. using a combination of two or more of the available media

9. To assure credibility and avoid hostility, the public relations man MUST

   A. make certain his message is truthful, not evasive or exaggerated
   B. make sure his message contains some dire consequence if ignored
   C. repeat the message often enough so that it cannot be ignored
   D. try to reach as many people and groups as possible

10. The public relations man MUST be prepared to assume that members of his audience

    A. may have developed attitudes toward his proposals --favorable, neutral, or unfavorable
    B. will be immediately hostile
    C. will consider his proposals with an open mind
    D. will invariably need an introduction to his subject

11. The one of the following statements that is CORRECT is:

    A. When a stupid question is asked of you by the public, it should be disregarded
    B. If you insist on formality between you and the public, the public will not be able to ask stupid questions that cannot be answered
    C. The public should be treated courteously, regardless of how stupid their questions may be
    D. You should explain to the public how stupid their questions are

3 (#1)

12. With regard to public relations, the MOST important item which should be emphasized in an employee training program is that   12._____

    A. each inspector is a public relations agent
    B. an inspector should give the public all the information it asks for
    C. it is better to make mistakes and give erroneous information than to tell the public that you do not know the correct answer to their problem
    D. public relations is so specialized a field that only persons specially trained in it should consider it

13. Members of the public frequently ask about departmental procedures.   13._____
    Of the following, it is BEST to

    A. advise the public to put the question in writing so, that he can get a proper formal reply
    B. refuse to answer because this is a confidential matter
    C. explain the procedure as briefly as possible
    D. attempt to avoid the issue by discussing other matters

14. The effectiveness of a public relations program in a public agency such as the authority is BEST indicated by the   14._____

    A. amount of mass media publicity favorable to the policies of the authority
    B. morale of those employees who directly serve the patrons of the authority
    C. public's understanding and support of the authority's program and policies
    D. number of complaints received by the authority from patrons using its facilities

15. In an attempt to improve public opinion about a certain idea, the BEST course of action for an agency to take would be to present the   15._____

    A. clearest statements of the idea even though the language is somewhat technical
    B. idea as the result of long-term studies
    C. idea in association with something familiar to most people
    D. idea as the viewpoint of the majority leaders

16. The fundamental factor in any agency's community relations program is   16._____

    A. an outline of the objectives
    B. relations with the media
    C. the everyday actions of the employees
    D. a well-planned supervisory program

17. The FUNDAMENTAL factor in the success of a community relations program is   17._____

    A. true commitment by the community
    B. true commitment by the administration
    C. a well-planned, systematic approach
    D. the actions of individuals in their contacts with the public

18. The statement below which is LEAST correct is: 18._____

    A. Because of selection standards, the supervisor frequently encounters problems resulting from subordinates' inability to express themselves in the language of the profession

B. Distortion of the meaning of a communication is usually brought about by a failure to use language that has a precise meaning to others
C. The term *filtering* is the distortion or dilution of content of a communication that occurs as information is passed from individual to individual
D. The complexity of the *communications net* will directly affect

19. Consider the following three statements that may or may not be CORRECT:
    I. In order to prevent the stifling of communications flow, supervisors should insist that employees use the formal communications network
    II. Two-way communications are faster and more accurate than one-way communications
    III. There is a direct correlation between the effectiveness of communications and the total setting in which they occur

    The choice below which MOST accurately describes the above statement is:

    A. All 3 are correct
    B. All 3 are incorrect
    C. More than one of the statements is correct
    D. Only one of the statements is correct

20. The statement below which is MOST inaccurate is:

    A. The supervisor's most important tool in learning whether or not he is communicating well is feedback
    B. Follow-up is essential if useful feedback is to be obtained
    C. Subordinates are entitled, as a matter of right, to explanations from management concerning the reasons for orders or directives
    D. A skilled supervisor is often able to use the grapevine to good advantage

21. *Since concurrence by those affected is not sought, this kind of communication can be issued with relative ease.* The kind of communication being referred to in this quotation is

    A. autocratic   B. democratic   C. directive   D. free-rein

22. The statement below which is LEAST correct is:

    A. Clarity is more important in oral communicating than in written since the readers of a written communication can read it over again
    B. Excessive use of abbreviations in written communications should be avoided
    C. Short sentences with simple words are preferred over complex sentences and difficult words in a written communication
    D. The *newspaper* style of writing ordinarily simplifies expression and facilitates understanding

23. Which one of the following is the MOST important factor for the department to consider in building a good public image?

    A. A good working relationship with the news media
    B. An efficient community relations program
    C. An efficient system for handling citizen complaints
    D. The proper maintenance of facilities and equipment
    E. The behavior of individuals in their contacts with the public

24. It has been said that the ability to communicate clearly and concisely is the MOST important single skill of the supervisor.
Consider the following statements:
    I. The adage, *Actions speak louder than words,* has NO application in superior/subordinate communications since good communications are accomplished with words
    II. The environment in which a communication takes place will *rarely* determine its effect
    III. Words are symbolic representations which must be associated with past experience or else they are meaningless

    The choice below which MOST accurately describes the above statements is:

    A. I, II and III are correct
    B. I and II are correct, but III is not
    C. I and III are correct, but II is not
    D. III is correct, but I and II are not
    E. I, II, and III are incorrect

25. According to expert opinion, the effectiveness of an organization is very dependent upon good upward, downward, and lateral communications. Lateral communications are most important to the activity of coordinating the efforts of organizational units. Before real communication can take place at any level, barriers to communication must be recognized, understood, and removed. Consider the following three statements:
    I. The *principal* barrier to good communications is a failure to establish empathy between sender and receiver
    II. The difference in status or rank between the sender and receiver of a communication may be a communications barrier
    III. Communications are easier if they travel upward from subordinate to superior

    The choice below which MOST accurately describes the above statements is:

    A. I, II and III are incorrect
    B. I and II are incorrect
    C. I, II, and III are correct
    D. I and II are correct
    E. I and III are incorrect

KEY (CORRECT ANSWERS)

1.	B	11.	C
2.	D	12.	A
3.	A	13.	C
4.	A	14.	C
5.	D	15.	C
6.	D	16.	C
7.	A	17.	D
8.	D	18.	A
9.	A	19.	D
10.	A	20.	C

21. A
22. A
23. E
24. D
25. E

———

EXAMINATION SECTION
TEST 1

DIRECTIONS: Each question or incomplete statement is followed by several suggested answers or completions. Select the one that BEST answers the question or completes the statement. *PRINT THE LETTER OF THE CORRECT ANSWER IN THE SPACE AT THE RIGHT.*

1. In public agencies, communications should be based PRIMARILY on a   1._____

    A. two-way flow from the top down and from the bottom up, most of which should be given in writing to avoid ambiguity
    B. multidirection flow among all levels and with outside persons
    C. rapid, internal one-way flow from the top down
    D. two-way flow of information, most of which should be given orally for purposes of clarity

2. In some organizations, changes in policy or procedures are often communicated by word   2._____
of mouth from supervisors to employees with no prior discussion or exchange of viewpoints with employees.
This procedure often produces employee dissatisfaction CHIEFLY because

    A. information is mostly unusable since a considerable amount of time is required to transmit information
    B. lower-level supervisors tend to be excessively concerned with minor details
    C. management has failed to seek employees' advice before making changes
    D. valuable staff time is lost between decision-making and the implementation of decisions

3. For good letter writing, you should try to visualize the person to whom you are writing,   3._____
especially if you know him.
Of the following rules, it is LEAST helpful in such visualization to think of

    A. the person's likes and dislikes, his concerns, and his needs
    B. what you would be likely to say if speaking in person
    C. what you would expect to be asked if speaking in person
    D. your official position in order to be certain that your words are proper

4. One approach to good informal letter writing is to make letters sound conversational.   4._____
All of the following practices will usually help to do this EXCEPT:

    A. If possible, use a style which is similar to the style used when speaking
    B. Substitute phrases for single words (e.g., *at the present time* for *now*)
    C. Use contractions of words (e.g., *you're* for *you are*)
    D. Use ordinary vocabulary when possible

5. All of the following rules will aid in producing clarity in report-writing EXCEPT: 5._____

    A. Give specific details or examples, if possible
    B. Keep related words close together in each sentence
    C. Present information in sequential order
    D. Put several thoughts or ideas in each paragraph

6. The one of the following statements about public relations which is MOST accurate is that
   A. in the long run, appearance gains better results than performance
   B. objectivity is decreased if outside public relations consultants are employed
   C. public relations is the responsibility of every employee
   D. public relations should be based on a formal publicity program

7. The form of communication which is usually considered to be MOST personally directed to the intended recipient is the
   A. brochure   B. film   C. letter   D. radio

8. In general, a document that presents an organization's views or opinions on a particular topic is MOST accurately known as a
   A. tear sheet
   B. position paper
   C. flyer
   D. journal

9. Assume that you have been asked to speak before an organization of persons who oppose a newly announced program in which you are involved. You feel tense about talking to this group.
   Which of the following rules generally would be MOST useful in gaining rapport when speaking before the audience?
   A. Impress them with your experience
   B. Stress all areas of disagreement
   C. Talk to the group as to one person
   D. Use formal grammar and language

10. An organization must have an effective public relations program since, at its best, public relations is a bridge to change.
    All of the following statements about communication and human behavior have validity EXCEPT:
    A. People are more likely to talk about controversial matters with like-minded people than with those holding other views
    B. The earlier an experience, the more powerful its effect since it influences how later experiences will be interpreted
    C. In periods of social tension, official sources gain increased believability
    D. Those who are already interested in a topic are the ones who are most open to receive new communications about it

11. An employee should be encouraged to talk easily and frankly when he is dealing with his supervisor.
    In order to encourage such free communication, it would be MOST appropriate for a supervisor to behave in a(n)
    A. sincere manner; assure the employee that you will deal with him honestly and openly
    B. official manner; you are a supervisor and must always act formally with subordinates

C. investigative manner; you must probe and question to get to a basis of trust
D. unemotional manner; the employee's emotions and background should play no part in your dealings with him

12. Research findings show that an increase in free communication within an agency GENERALLY results in which one of the following?

    A. Improved morale and productivity
    B. Increased promotional opportunities
    C. An increase in authority
    D. A spirit of honesty

13. Assume that you are a supervisor and your superiors have given you a new-type procedure to be followed.
    Before passing this information on to your subordinates, the one of the following actions that you should take FIRST is to

    A. ask your superiors to send out a memorandum to the entire staff
    B. clarify the procedure in your own mind
    C. set up a training course to provide instruction on the new procedure
    D. write a memorandum to your subordinates

14. Communication is necessary for an organization to be effective.
    The one of the following which is LEAST important for most communication systems is that

    A. messages are sent quickly and directly to the person who needs them to operate
    B. information should be conveyed understandably and accurately
    C. the method used to transmit information should be kept secret so that security can be maintained
    D. senders of messages must know how their messages are received and acted upon

15. Which one of the following is the CHIEF advantage of listening willingly to subordinates and encouraging them to talk freely and honestly?
    It

    A. reveals to supervisors the degree to which ideas that are passed down are accepted by subordinates
    B. reduces the participation of subordinates in the operation of the department
    C. encourages subordinates to try for promotion
    D. enables supervisors to learn more readily what the *grapevine* is saying

16. A supervisor may be informed through either oral or written reports.
    Which one of the following is an ADVANTAGE of using oral reports?

    A. There is no need for a formal record of the report.
    B. An exact duplicate of the report is not easily transmitted to others.
    C. A good oral report requires little time for preparation.
    D. An oral report involves two-way communication between a subordinate and his supervisor.

17. Of the following, the MOST important reason why supervisors should communicate effectively with the public is to

    A. improve the public's understanding of information that is important for them to know
    B. establish a friendly relationship
    C. obtain information about the kinds of people who come to the agency
    D. convince the public that services are adequate

18. Supervisors should generally NOT use phrases like *too hard, too easy,* and *a lot* PRINCIPALLY because such phrases

    A. may be offensive to some minority groups
    B. are too informal
    C. mean different things to different people
    D. are difficult to remember

19. The ability to communicate clearly and concisely is an important element in effective leadership.
    Which of the following statements about oral and written communication is GENERALLY true?

    A. Oral communication is more time-consuming.
    B. Written communication is more likely to be misinterpreted.
    C. Oral communication is useful only in emergencies.
    D. Written communication is useful mainly when giving information to fewer than twenty people.

20. Rumors can often have harmful and disruptive effects on an organization.
    Which one of the following is the BEST way to prevent rumors from becoming a problem?

    A. Refuse to act on rumors, thereby making them less believable.
    B. Increase the amount of information passed along by the *grapevine*.
    C. Distribute as much factual information as possible.
    D. Provide training in report writing.

21. Suppose that a subordinate asks you about a rumor he has heard. The rumor deals with a subject which your superiors consider *confidential*.
    Which of the following BEST describes how you should answer the subordinate?
    Tell

    A. the subordinate that you don't make the rules and that he should speak to higher ranking officials
    B. the subordinate that you will ask your superior for information
    C. him only that you cannot comment on the matter
    D. him the rumor is not true

22. Supervisors often find it difficult to *get their message across* when instructing newly appointed employees in their various duties.
    The MAIN reason for this is generally that the

A. duties of the employees have increased
B. supervisor is often so expert in his area that he fails to see it from the learner's point of view
C. supervisor adapts his instruction to the slowest learner in the group
D. new employees are younger, less concerned with job security and more interested in fringe benefits

23. Assume that you are discussing a job problem with an employee under your supervision. During the discussion, you see that the man's eyes are turning away from you and that he is not paying attention.
In order to get the man's attention, you should FIRST

    A. ask him to look you in the eye
    B. talk to him about sports
    C. tell him he is being very rude
    D. change your tone of voice

23.____

24. As a supervisor, you may find it necessary to conduct meetings with your subordinates. Of the following, which would be MOST helpful in assuring that a meeting accomplishes the purpose for which it was called?

    A. Give notice of the conclusions you would like to reach at the start of the meeting.
    B. Delay the start of the meeting until everyone is present.
    C. Write down points to be discussed in proper sequence.
    D. Make sure everyone is clear on whatever conclusions have been reached and on what must be done after the meeting.

24.____

25. Every supervisor will occasionally be called upon to deliver a reprimand to a subordinate. If done properly, this can greatly help an employee improve his performance.
Which one of the following is NOT a good practice to follow when giving a reprimand?

    A. Maintain your composure and temper.
    B. Reprimand a subordinate in the presence of other employees so they can learn the same lesson.
    C. Try to understand why the employee was not able to perform satisfactorily.
    D. Let your knowledge of the man involved determine the exact nature of the reprimand.

25.____

KEY (CORRECT ANSWERS)

1.	C	11.	A
2.	B	12.	A
3.	D	13.	B
4.	B	14.	C
5.	D	15.	A
6.	C	16.	D
7.	C	17.	A
8.	B	18.	C
9.	C	19.	B
10.	C	20.	C

21. B
22. B
23. D
24. D
25. B

TEST 2

DIRECTIONS: Each question or incomplete statement is followed by several suggested answers or completions. Select the one that BEST answers the question or completes the statement. *PRINT THE LETTER OF THE CORRECT ANSWER IN THE SPACE AT THE RIGHT.*

1. Usually one thinks of communication as a single step, essentially that of transmitting an idea.
Actually, however, this is only part of a total process, the FIRST step of which should be

    A. the prompt dissemination of the idea to those who may be affected by it
    B. motivating those affected to take the required action
    C. clarifying the idea in one's own mind
    D. deciding to whom the idea is to be communicated

    1.____

2. Research studies on patterns of informal communication have concluded that most individuals in a group tend to be passive recipients of news, while a few make it their business to spread it around in an organization.
With this conclusion in mind, it would be MOST correct for the supervisor to attempt to identify these few individuals and

    A. give them the complete facts on important matters in advance of others
    B. inform the other subordinates of the identify of these few individuals so that their influence may be minimized
    C. keep them straight on the facts on important matters
    D. warn them to cease passing along any information to others

    2.____

3. The one of the following which is the PRINCIPAL advantage of making an oral report is that it

    A. affords an immediate opportunity for two-way communication between the subordinate and superior
    B. is an easy method for the superior to use in transmitting information to others of equal rank
    C. saves the time of all concerned
    D. permits more precise pinpointing of praise or blame by means of follow-up questions by the superior

    3.____

4. An agency may sometimes undertake a public relations program of a defensive nature.
With reference to the use of defensive public relations, it would be MOST correct to state that it

    A. is bound to be ineffective since defensive statements, even though supported by factual data, can never hope to even partly overcome the effects of prior unfavorable attacks
    B. proves that the agency has failed to establish good relationships with newspapers, radio stations, or other means of publicity
    C. shows that the upper echelons of the agency have failed to develop sound public relations procedures and techniques
    D. is sometimes required to aid morale by protecting the agency from unjustified criticism and misunderstanding of policies or procedures

    4.____

5. Of the following factors which contribute to possible undesirable public attitudes towards an agency, the one which is MOST susceptible to being changed by the efforts of the individual employee in an organization is that

   A. enforcement of unpopular regulations has offended many individuals
   B. the organization itself has an unsatisfactory reputation
   C. the public is not interested in agency matters
   D. there are many errors in judgment committed by individual subordinates

6. It is not enough for an agency's services to be of a high quality; attention must also be given to the acceptability of these services to the general public.
   This statement is GENERALLY

   A. *false;* a superior quality of service automatically wins public support
   B. *true;* the agency cannot generally progress beyond the understanding and support of the public
   C. *false;* the acceptance by the public of agency services determines their quality
   D. *true;* the agency is generally unable to engage in any effective enforcement activity without public support

7. Sustained agency participation in a program sponsored by a community organization is MOST justified when

   A. the achievement of agency objectives in some area depends partly on the activity of this organization
   B. the community organization is attempting to widen the base of participation in all community affairs
   C. the agency is uncertain as to what the community wants
   D. there is an obvious lack of good leadership in a newly formed community organization

8. Of the following, the LEAST likely way in which a records system may serve a supervisor is in

   A. developing a sympathetic and cooperative public attitude toward the agency
   B. improving the quality of supervision by permitting a check on the accomplishment of subordinates
   C. permit a precise prediction of the exact incidences in specific categories for the following year
   D. helping to take the guesswork out of the distribution of the agency

9. Assuming that the *grapevine* in any organization is virtually indestructible, the one of the following which it is MOST important for management to understand is:

   A. What is being spread by means of the *grapevine* and the reason for spreading it
   B. What is being spread by means of the *grapevine* and how it is being spread
   C. Who is involved in spreading the information that is on the *grapevine*
   D. Why those who are involved in spreading the information are doing so

10. When the supervisor writes a report concerning an investigation to which he has been assigned, it should be LEAST intended to provide

    A. a permanent official record of relevant information gathered
    B. a summary of case findings limited to facts which tend to indicate the guilt of a suspect
    C. a statement of the facts on which higher authorities may base a corrective or disciplinary action
    D. other investigators with information so that they may continue with other phases of the investigation

11. In survey work, questionnaires rather than interviews are sometimes used.
    The one of the following which is a DISADVANTAGE of the questionnaire method as compared with the interview is the

    A. difficulty of accurately interpreting the results
    B. problem of maintaining anonymity of the participant
    C. fact that it is relatively uneconomical
    D. requirement of special training for the distribution of questionnaires

12. In his contacts with the public, an employee should attempt to create a good climate of support for his agency. This statement is GENERALLY

    A. *false;* such attempts are clearly beyond the scope of his responsibility
    B. *true;* employees of an agency who come in contact with the public have the opportunity to affect public relations
    C. *false;* such activity should be restricted to supervisors trained in public relations techniques
    D. *true;* the future expansion of the agency depends to a great extent on continued public support of the agency

13. The repeated use by a supervisor of a call for volunteers to get a job done is objectionable MAINLY because it

    A. may create a feeling of animosity between the volunteers and the non-volunteers
    B. may indicate that the supervisor is avoiding responsibility for making assignments which will be most productive
    C. is an indication that the supervisor is not familiar with the individual capabilities of his men
    D. is unfair to men who, for valid reasons, do not, or cannot volunteer

14. Of the following statements concerning subordinates' expressions to a supervisor of their opinions and feelings concerning work situations, the one which is MOST correct is that

    A. by listening and responding to such expressions the supervisor encourages the development of complaints
    B. the lack of such expressions should indicate to the supervisor that there is a high level of job satisfaction
    C. the more the supervisor listens to and responds to such expressions, the more he demonstrates lack of supervisory ability
    D. by listening and responding to such expressions, the supervisor will enable many subordinates to understand and solve their own problems on the job

15. In attempting to motivate employees, rewards are considered preferable to punishment PRIMARILY because

    A. punishment seldom has any effect on human behavior
    B. punishment usually results in decreased production
    C. supervisors find it difficult to punish
    D. rewards are more likely to result in willing cooperation

16. In an attempt to combat the low morale in his organization, a high-level supervisor publicized an *open-door* policy to allow employees who wished to do so to come to him with their complaints.
    Which of the following is LEAST likely to account for the fact that no employee came in with a complaint?

    A. Employees are generally reluctant to go over the heads of their immediate supervisors.
    B. The employees did not feel that management would help them.
    C. The low morale was not due to complaints associated with the job.
    D. The employees felt that they had more to lose than to gain.

17. It is MOST desirable to use written instructions rather than oral instructions for a particular job when

    A. a mistake on the job will not be serious
    B. the job can be completed in a short time
    C. there is no need to explain the job minutely
    D. the job involves many details

18. If you receive a telephone call regarding a matter which your office does not handle, you should FIRST

    A. give the caller the telephone number of the proper office so that he can dial again
    B. offer to transfer the caller to the proper office
    C. suggest that the caller re-dial since he probably dialed incorrectly
    D. tell the caller he has reached the wrong office and then hang up

19. When you answer the telephone, the MOST important reason for identifying yourself and your organization is to

    A. give the caller time to collect his or her thoughts
    B. impress the caller with your courtesy
    C. inform the caller that he or she has reached the right number
    D. set a business-like tone at the beginning of the conversation

20. As soon as you pick up the phone, a very angry caller begins immediately to complain about city agencies and *red tape*. He says that he has been shifted to two or three different offices. It turns out that he is seeking information which is not immediately available to you. You believe you know, however, where it can be found. Which of the following actions is the BEST one for you to take?

    A. To eliminate all confusion, suggest that the caller write the agency stating explicitly what he wants.
    B. Apologize by telling the caller how busy city agencies now are, but also tell him directly that you do not have the information he needs.

5 (#2)

    C. Ask for the caller's telephone number and assure him you will call back after you have checked further.
    D. Give the caller the name and telephone number of the person who might be able to help, but explain that you are not positive he will get results.

21. Which of the following approaches usually provides the BEST communication in the objectives and values of a new program which is to be introduced? 21.____

    A. A general written description of the program by the program manager for review by those who share responsibility
    B. An effective verbal presentation by the program manager to those affected
    C. Development of the plan and operational approach in carrying out the program by the program manager assisted by his key subordinates
    D. Development of the plan by the program manager's supervisor

22. What is the BEST approach for introducing change? 22.____
A

    A. combination of written and also verbal communication to all personnel affected by the change
    B. general bulletin to all personnel
    C. meeting pointing out all the values of the new approach
    D. written directive to key personnel

23. Of the following, committees are BEST used for 23.____

    A. advising the head of the organization
    B. improving functional work
    C. making executive decisions
    D. making specific planning decisions

24. An effective discussion leader is one who 24.____

    A. announces the problem and his preconceived solution at the start of the discussion
    B. guides and directs the discussion according to pre-arranged outline
    C. interrupts or corrects confused participants to save time
    D. permits anyone to say anything at anytime

25. The human relations movement in management theory is basically concerned with 25.____

    A. counteracting employee unrest
    B. eliminating the *time and motion* man
    C. interrelationships among individuals in organizations
    D. the psychology of the worker

KEY (CORRECT ANSWERS)

1.	C	11.	A
2.	C	12.	B
3.	A	13.	B
4.	D	14.	D
5.	D	15.	D
6.	B	16.	C
7.	A	17.	D
8.	C	18.	B
9.	A	19.	C
10.	B	20.	C

21. C
22. A
23. A
24. B
25. C

———

EXAMINATION SECTION
TEST 1

DIRECTIONS: Each question or incomplete statement is followed by several suggested answers or completions. Select the one that BEST answers the question or completes the statement. *PRINT THE LETTER OF THE CORRECT ANSWER IN THE SPACE AT THE RIGHT.*

1. The model of public relations practice MOST commonly used by government agencies is the _____ model.

    A. press agentry/publicity
    B. public information
    C. two-way asymmetric
    D. two-way symmetric

2. Each of the following is one of the four primary areas of government-related public relations practice EXCEPT

    A. politics
    B. special interests inside government
    C. lobbying
    D. public affairs

3. Which of the following statements is considered to be one of the learning principles associated with consumer behaviors?

    A. It is easier to recall an appeal than to recognize it.
    B. Appeals made in exhaustive, momentary bursts of information are most effective.
    C. Unique messages are remembered more completely than others.
    D. Unpleasant appeals are usually not learned as well as pleasant ones.

4. Which phase of the diffusion cycle of persuasive information would occur FIRST?

    A. Information
    B. Adoption
    C. Reinforcement
    D. Awareness

5. Which of the following is a guideline associated with researching public relations campaigns associated with television or radio broadcasting?

    A. Design surveys to include primarily open-ended questions
    B. Attempt to cover the largest area possible
    C. Collect information by telephone or face-to-face interviews rather than by mail
    D. Gather information about subject's friends and family members, to conserve time

6. In which persuasive strategy is the cost-effectiveness of message repetition MOST problematic?

    A. Personality appeal
    B. Cognitive
    C. Stimulus-response
    D. Motivational

7. Which of the following is NOT one of the basic ideas behind the effort to influence public opinion?

    A. Reliability is difficult to assess
    B. Words, rather than events, are most likely to affect opinion
    C. Demands for action are a usual response
    D. Self-interest figures heavily into public involvement

8. _____ is categorized specifically as a *self-esteem* need that should be considered by the formers of a message.

   A. Knowledge
   B. Acceptance
   C. Intellectual curiosity
   D. Peace

9. Which of the following is NOT one of the personal characteristics considered necessary for a public relations practitioner?

   A. Intuition
   B. Specialized cultural background
   C. Training in the social sciences
   D. Objectivity

10. According to the basic principles of public relations, _____ is the sole criterion by which a public relations professional should be measured.

    A. versatility
    B. objectivity
    C. ethical performance
    D. demonstrated influence

11. Which method for determining client charges for public relations services is considered to be the RISKIEST?

    A. Hourly fee
    B. Fee for services and out-of-pocket expenses
    C. Fixed fee
    D. Retainer

12. According to the conditional probability theory of message receptiveness, the _____ public is among the secondary, rather than primary, group to target with a message.

    A. aware
    B. active
    C. latent
    D. latent/aware

13. The Public Relations Society of America's Code of Professional Standards defines political public relations as relating to each of the following EXCEPT the counseling of

    A. candidates or political organizations
    B. clients in connection with the client's relationship with government, with the purpose of influencing legislation
    C. media personnel who want to learn more about a candidate or political organization's record
    D. holders of public office

14. Which of the following is considered by public relations businesses to be a chargeable expense?

    A. Meetings with clients to prepare account material
    B. Maintaining contacts with media representatives
    C. Meetings with staff and other group conferences related to public relations business
    D. Preparation of materials for potential clients

15. Of the steps in a problem-oriented public relations campaign listed below, which would occur FIRST? 15.____

    A. Determine communications strategy
    B. Evaluation of problem's impact
    C. Development of organizational strategy
    D. Deciding upon tactics

16. Which function of a public relations practitioner involves analyzing problems and opportunities, as well as assigning responsibilities to appropriate personnel? 16.____

    A. Programming   B. Relationships
    C. Research and evaluation   D. Production

17. Which of the following is an advantage associated with the use of television as a medium for public relations communication? 17.____

    A. Good product identification
    B. Almost unlimited time allotment
    C. The creation of opportunities for consumer referral
    D. Low production costs

18. Which persuasive strategy is designed specifically for *outer-directed* people? 18.____

    A. Personality appeal   B. Social appeal
    C. Stimulus-response   D. Cognitive

19. The _____ model of public relations practice is characterized by an attempt to persuade the public to adopt the organization's point-of-view, 19.____

    A. press agentry/publicity   B. public information
    C. two-way asymmetric   D. two-way symmetric

20. Which of the following is one of the *laws* of public opinion? 20.____

    A. Opinion is basically determined by self-interest.
    B. Generally, public opinion is useful for the anticipation of emergencies.
    C. Opinion is usually sustainable through repetitive appeals.
    D. Generally, opinion is not sensitive to important events

21. In terms of psychographic research, which of the following personality types would be considered *outer-directed?* 21.____

    A. Sustainers   B. Achievers
    C. Experimentals   D. Survivors

22. Which of the following is a disadvantage associated with the use of radio as a medium for public relations communication? 22.____

    A. Time restrictions
    B. Neglect of local markets
    C. Relatively high production costs
    D. Difficulty in altering copy

23. Which of the following statements is NOT one of the basic principles of public relations practice? 23.____

    A. Public relations is primarily a service-oriented profession.
    B. Practitioners depend heavily on scientific public opinion research.
    C. Public relations is concerned not so much with reality as with the public's perception of reality.
    D. Practitioners depend largely on theories and practices of the social sciences.

24. The communication theory which claims that the stability of a society is dependent upon its organization is 24.____

    A. symbolic interactionism
    B. structural functionalism
    C. sociocultural paradigm
    D. social conflict

25. Which of the following types of measurements would be used to determine the ethical dimensions of a message? 25.____

    A. Powerful-weak
    B. Biased-unbiased
    C. Easy-difficult
    D. Active-passive

KEY (CORRECT ANSWERS)

1. B		11. C	
2. B		12. B	
3. C		13. C	
4. D		14. A	
5. C		15. B	
6. C		16. A	
7. B		17. A	
8. A		18. A	
9. B		19. C	
10. C		20. A	

21. B
22. A
23. C
24. B
25. B

TEST 2

DIRECTIONS: Each question or incomplete statement is followed by several suggested answers or completions. Select the one that BEST answers the question or completes the statement. *PRINT THE LETTER OF THE CORRECT ANSWER IN THE SPACE AT THE RIGHT.*

1. A typical public relations practitioner spends MOST of his/her professional time with   1.____

    A. lobbying
    B. media contacts/press conferences
    C. radio/television appearances
    D. speechmaking

2. Which of the following is an element of off-premise community relations, as practiced by the administration of an organization?   2.____

    A. Care for the handicapped and aged
    B. Open houses
    C. Offering free consultations
    D. Community bulletin boards

3. Each of the following is an explanation for the typically large budgets associated with the production of an annual report EXCEPT   3.____

    A. that it is the primary means by which most organizations communicate with the public
    B. high deadline pressures
    C. increasing regulation by the Securities and Exchange Commission
    D. that few other public relations methods practiced by the organization require much funding

4. What is the term for a speech written so that several speakers can deliver it to different audiences with only minor variations?   4.____

    A. Semantic   B. Basic   C. Pattern   D. Quota

5. Which of the following is NOT a reason for using the *inverted pyramid* style when writing public relations news releases?   5.____

    A. Good for hurried readers
    B. Will draw attention in opening lines
    C. Gives writer more room to present an idea or event
    D. Can usually be edited or cut without much loss of important information

6. Which of the following is NOT an objective of government information efforts?   6.____

    A. Explain agency techniques in a way that invites input from citizens
    B. Provide citizen feedback to government administrators
    C. Implement changes in the policies of government agencies, aligning with public opinion
    D. Communicate the work of government agencies

7. The model of public relations practice MOST commonly used by highly-regulated business, such as the telephone industry, is the _____ model.

   A. press agentry/publicity B. public information
   C. two-way asymmetric D. two-way symmetric

8. Which of the following is an advantage associated with the use of magazines as media for public relations communication?

   A. Domination of local markets
   B. Immediacy of message
   C. Nonselective targeting of audience
   D. Access to affluent consumers

9. Which persuasive strategy is designed specifically for people who have no negative preconceptions about the target behavior?

   A. Personality appeal B. Social appeal
   C. Motivational D. Cognitive

10. The pursuit of management objectives through supervision, delegation of authority, and work assignments is called the _____ function.

    A. line B. transfer
    C. staff D. institutional

11. Which of the following is NOT usually considered part of the necessary contents of internal publications?

    A. News stories B. Employee opinion forum
    C. Feature stories D. Items of record

12. In communications theory, the person or group that receives a message is known as the

    A. decoder B. gatekeeper
    C. encoder D. planter

13. When scheduling the preparation of public service announcements, APPROXIMATELY how much time should be set aside to allow for the choice of a cause or topic? _____ hours.

    A. 1-2 B. 2-4 C. 4-12 D. 8-16

14. Which of the following is NOT one of the *laws* of public opinion?

    A. People have more opinions with respect to goals than with respect to the means by which to achieve them.
    B. Public opinion is based more on information than desire.
    C. When opinion is not solidly structured, an accomplished fact tends to shift opinion in the accepted direction.
    D. Opinion is primarily reactive rather than proactive.

15. When a public relations practitioner selects opinion leaders to be interviewed, in order to insure the success of a campaign, this is known as _____ sampling.

    A. probability B. internal
    C. quota D. purposive

16. Which of the following is considered by public relations businesses to be a nonchargeable expense?

    A. Preparation of visual materials used in presentations
    B. Off-hours time spent with client personnel on client matters
    C. Professional development activities such as seminars
    D. Photographic assignments

17. Which of the following is NOT considered one of the ethical guidelines for people working in political public relations?
    Members shall not

    A. distribute advertising or publicity information which in unlabeled as to its source
    B. make gifts to influence decisions of voters or legislators
    C. engage in the inherently biased practice of partisan advocacy
    D. through information known to be misleading, intentionally injure the public reputation of the opposing candidate

18. A publicist who delivers new releases to media offices and urges their use is known as a(n)

    A. planter   B. encoder
    C. gatekeeper   D. booker

19. According to the conditional probability theory of message receptiveness, the most cost-effective for message distribution is a(n) _____ public characterized by _____ behaviors.

    A. latent/aware; constrained
    B. latent; routine
    C. active; problem-facing
    D. inactive; fatalistic

20. The communication theory which claims that the media's constructs of reality ultimately result in a society's individual and collective creations of reality is called

    A. symbolic interactionism
    B. social conflict
    C. evolutionary perspective
    D. psychodynamic model

21. Which of the following is an advantage associated with the use of direct mailing as a medium for public relations communication?

    A. Relaxed regulation of content
    B. Inexpensive
    C. Selectivity of target audience
    D. Consistency of mailing lists

22. Each of the following elements in a persuasive message is considered essential to provoking a response EXCEPT

    A. familiarity and trust   B. spirited challenge
    C. identification   D. suggestion of action

23. Which function of a public relations practitioner requires background knowledge of art, layout, and photography?

    A. Programming
    B. Information
    C. Research and evaluation
    D. Production

24. In researching public relations campaigns associated with television or radio broadcasting, what is generally considered to be the upper limit for the cross-section of the public necessary to provide an adequate information sample?

    A. 100   B. 500   C. 1,000   D. 5,000

25. Of the steps in scheduling an annual report listed below, which would occur FIRST?

    A. Producing copy
    B. Assigning work
    C. Clearing material recommendations
    D. Production

KEY (CORRECT ANSWERS)

1.	B	11.	B
2.	A	12.	A
3.	D	13.	C
4.	C	14.	D
5.	C	15.	B
6.	C	16.	C
7.	D	17.	C
8.	D	18.	A
9.	D	19.	A
10.	A	20.	A

21. C
22. B
23. D
24. C
25. B

EXAMINATION SECTION
TEST 1

DIRECTIONS: Each question or incomplete statement is followed by several suggested answers or completions. Select the one that BEST answers the question or completes the statement. *PRINT THE LETTER OF THE CORRECT ANSWER IN THE SPACE AT THE RIGHT.*

1. Each of the following is one of the first considerations public relations practitioners should make when selecting the appropriate medium for message distribution EXCEPT

    A. target audience
    B. date at which audience needs to be reached
    C. possible combinations of media
    D. costs

    1.____

2. Which phase of the diffusion cycle of persuasive information would occur LAST?

    A. Evaluation B. Trial
    C. Awareness D. Adoption

    2.____

3. Which of the following is NOT considered to be one of the important psychological dimensions of public opinion?

    A. Intensity B. Duration C. Direction D. Breadth

    3.____

4. The _____ persuasion model is specifically designed to study the fact that an effective message is a message that causes a desired behavior from a person.

    A. symbolic interactionism
    B. structural functionalism
    C. sociocultural paradigm
    D. psychodynamic

    4.____

5. The tryout of a public relations message on a small audience before general distribution is referred to as a

    A. release B. pilot C. hype D. plant

    5.____

6. Which of the following is NOT a title name typically held by government public relations practitioners?

    A. Public information officer
    B. Press secretary
    C. Director of public affairs
    D. Public relations representative

    6.____

7. Which persuasive strategy involves creating a need or stimulating a desire?

    A. Cognitive B. Social appeal
    C. Stimulus-response D. Motivational

    7.____

8. Which of the following is an advantage associated with the use of point-of-purchase displays as a medium for public relations communication?

    8.____

A. Low unit cost
B. Creative flexibility
C. Involvement of dealer as partner in display
D. Short production time

9. The _____ model of public relations practice is MOST commonly used by businesses in highly competitive markets?

   A. press agentry/publicity
   B. public information
   C. two-way asymmetric
   D. two-way symmetric

10. Which of the following types of measurements would be used to determine the potency dimensions of a message?

    A. Loud-soft
    B. Interesting-uninteresting
    C. Easy-difficult
    D. Active-passive

11. A publicist whose assignment is to place clients with prominent public events is known as a(n)

    A. booker
    B. planter
    C. gatekeeper
    D. agenda-setter

12. Which of the following is considered a rule for executives or public relations representatives being publicly interviewed?

    A. Use expert talk for credibility
    B. Offer to help reporter in the future
    C. Avoid touchy questions
    D. Avoid off-the-record remarks

13. Which of the following is considered by public relations businesses to be a *nonchargeable* expense?

    A. Interviews, surveys, and placement of materials
    B. The supervision of mailing and distribution of releases
    C. Social activities with clients
    D. Travel time

14. Which of the following is NOT considered to be one of the learning principles associated with consumer behaviors?

    A. Appeals made over an extended period of time are most effective.
    B. Repetition is more effective when related to satisfaction and belongingness.
    C. Knowledge of results increases learning of a message.
    D. Learning a new pattern of behavior often reinforces the patterns already developed.

15. Each of the following is an objective of most public relations organizations (i.e., the Council for Advancement and Support of Education) related to schools and colleges EXCEPT

    A. developing gift and expenditure standards
    B. direct recruitment for athletics and other extracurricular programs
    C. improving the communication of university research to the public
    D. helping minority leaders at institutions to advance their careers

16. _____ is considered a propaganda technique.

    A. Social validation   B. Transfer
    C. Suggestion of action   D. Clarification

17. Of the steps in a problem-oriented public relations campaign listed below, which would occur LAST?

    A. Determine communications strategy
    B. Evaluation of problem's impact
    C. Development of organizational strategy
    D. Deciding upon tactics

18. An organization's image is conveyed to the public and evaluated in each of the following areas EXCEPT

    A. financial responsibility
    B. ability to form public policy
    C. ethics
    D. social responsibility

19. Which of the following statements does NOT reflect a public relations principle used to help organizations to maintain favorable public opinion?

    A. The economic and social stability of an organization is dependent upon the attitudes of the public within its operational environment.
    B. Technology should be avoided at all costs to avoid distancing the organization from the public.
    C. An organization's management of communications is essential to its ultimate ability to adjust to changes necessary for longevity.
    D. All individuals have the right to information about pending decisions relating to them or their welfare.

20. Which communication theory claims that a society's groups have competing needs and interests?

    A. Evolutionary perspective
    B. Structural functionalism
    C. Sociocultural paradigm
    D. Social conflict

21. _____ is a disadvantage associated with the use of pamphlets and booklets as a medium for public relations communication.

    A. Poor color reproduction
    B. The lack of opportunity for consumer referral
    C. Difficulty in measuring effectiveness
    D. Presentation of nonspecific messages

22. In terms of psychographic research, which of the following personality types would be considered inner-directed?

    A. Achievers   B. Emulators
    C. Need-driven   D. Belongers

23. According to the conditional probability theory of message receptiveness, which type of public is the MOST cost-effective for message distribution?
A(n) _____ public characterized by _____.

    A. latent; constrained behaviors
    B. active; routine behaviors
    C. active; problem-facing behaviors
    D. aware; problem-facing behaviors

24. Which of the following is NOT typically one of the problems associated with an organization's internal publications?

    A. Too much space devoted to coverage of negative issues
    B. Little attempt to show how departments inter-relate
    C. Too office-oriented
    D. Not adequately funded

25. The type of survey in which every member of the targeted audience has a chance of being selected for questioning is the _____ sample.

    A. quota
    B. purposive
    C. probability
    D. social

KEY (CORRECT ANSWERS)

1.	C	11.	A
2.	D	12.	B
3.	B	13.	C
4.	D	14.	D
5.	B	15.	B
6.	D	16.	B
7.	D	17.	D
8.	B	18.	B
9.	C	19.	B
10.	A	20.	D

21. C
22. C
23. D
24. A
25. C

TEST 2

DIRECTIONS: Each question or incomplete statement is followed by several suggested answers or completions. Select the one that BEST answers the question or completes the statement. *PRINT THE LETTER OF THE CORRECT ANSWER IN THE SPACE AT THE RIGHT.*

1. Increasing _____ is NOT a factor leading to the growth of the governmental information effort. 1.____

   A. citizen demand
   B. complexity of society
   C. rural population
   D. public scrutiny

2. When scheduling the preparation of public service announcements, APPROXIMATELY how much time should be set aside for the on-set shooting of the spot? 2.____

   A. 2-4 hours
   B. 4-8 hours
   C. 8-14 hours
   D. 2-3 days

3. Which of the following types of studies is used to measure audience attitudes before and after a public relations campaign? 3.____

   A. Quota sampling
   B. Benchmark study
   C. Copy testing
   D. Retrieval study

4. Which of the following is NOT a role of the public relations person during an interview? 4.____

   A. Preparer
   B. Questioner
   C. Facilitator
   D. Clarifier

5. A review to determine public relations material and its relation to the target audience is 5.____

   A. probability sampling
   B. issues management
   C. a communication audit
   D. an institutional advertisement

6. Each of the following is a guideline for publicity photographs EXCEPT 6.____

   A. always keep the number of subjects above three
   B. keep the background neutral
   C. position subjects close together
   D. high contrast

7. The tendency of survey respondents to offer socially *correct* answers rather than ones disclosing their true opinions is known as 7.____

   A. courtesy bias
   B. transfer
   C. encoding
   D. flacking

8. Which of the following is a problem specific to the practice of international public relations? 8.____

   A. The containment of crises
   B. Difficulty in monitoring potentially adverse situations
   C. An awkwardly long chain of command
   D. Difficulty in maintaining a favorable climate for operations

9. Which persuasive strategy is MOST often used in an attempt to alleviate conditions for the poor and needy?

    A. Cognitive
    B. Social appeal
    C. Stimulus-response
    D. Motivational

10. The model of public relations practice MOST likely to involve withholding information from the public is the _____ model.

    A. press agentry/publicity
    B. public information
    C. two-way asymmetric
    D. two-way symmetric

11. In relation to social services, public relations techniques are considered essential to each of the following practices EXCEPT

    A. personnel
    B. client services
    C. fund-raising
    D. enlistment of volunteers

12. Of the steps in scheduling an annual report listed below, which would occur LAST?

    A. Producing copy
    B. Assigning work
    C. Clearing material recommendations
    D. Production

13. Public relations organizations working in the United States for other nations can expect to perform each of the following tasks EXCEPT

    A. advance political objectives
    B. assist in communications in the country's own language
    C. counsel the country about possible United States reactions to activities
    D. help modify laws and regulations inhibiting client's activities in the United States

14. Which method for determining client charges is MOST commonly used by public relations practitioners?

    A. Hourly fee
    B. Fee for services and out-of-pocket expenses
    C. Fixed fee
    D. Retainer

15. What is the term for the survey technique in which multiple samplings drawn from the same population are studied longitudinally and then compared or contrasted?

    A. Census
    B. Cohort study
    C. Bridge study
    D. Coincidental interview

16. The communication theory which claims that social change follows a set of natural laws is called

    A. evolutionary perspective
    B. structural functionalism
    C. sociocultural paradigm
    D. social conflict

17. Which of the following is NOT an advantage associated with electronically communicated information?

    A. Exists as part of people's everyday lives
    B. Often shows events happening, as well as reports them
    C. Immediacy of message
    D. Can selectively reach desired audiences

18. Which of the following is an element of off-premise community relations, as practiced by the administration of an organization?

    A. Talks to area organizations
    B. Anniversary celebrations
    C. Corporate disclosure
    D. Tables for fundraising

19. The pursuit of management objectives through suggestions, recommendation, and advice is the _____ function.

    A. line   B. transfer
    C. transfer   D. institutional

20. A typical public relations practitioner spends the LEAST amount of his/her professional time with

    A. lobbying
    B. media contacts/press conferences
    C. radio/television appearances
    D. meetings with outside groups

21. Which of the following is NOT a rule for executives or public relations representatives being publicly interviewed?

    A. Encourage hypothetical questions
    B. Avoid injecting yourself into the process during the actual interview
    C. Admit to not knowing the answer to some questions
    D. Answer questions that are public record

22. Which of the following is NOT generally considered a factor in determining the difficulty of an organization's internal communications?

    A. More sources such as television to divert workers' attention
    B. Increasing two-income families dilute one's interest in his/her job
    C. Increase in childbirth rate has produced competing responsibilities
    D. Increasing mobility of workers

23. The selection of a group to be polled that matches the characteristics of the entire audience is known as _____ sampling.

    A. probability   B. internal
    C. quota   D. purposive

24. The MOST important consideration in planning the composition of an annual report is

    A. scheduling   B. photography assignments
    C. distribution   D. printing procedures

25. Which of the following is NOT an objective of government information efforts? 25.___
    A. Represent the public and present its interests to representatives
    B. Advise government management on how best to communicate a decision or program
    C. Lobby for legislation supported by public opinion polls
    D. Educate administrators and bureaucrats about the role of mass media

---

KEY (CORRECT ANSWERS)

1.	C	11.	A
2.	C	12.	D
3.	B	13.	B
4.	C	14.	B
5.	C	15.	B
6.	A	16.	A
7.	A	17.	D
8.	C	18.	C
9.	B	19.	C
10.	A	20.	A

21.	A
22.	C
23.	C
24.	A
25.	C

EXAMINATION SECTION
TEST 1

DIRECTIONS: Each question or incomplete statement is followed by several suggested answers or completions. Select the one that BEST answers the question or completes the statement. *PRINT THE LETTER OF THE CORRECT ANSWER IN THE SPACE AT THE RIGHT.*

1. You are preparing a press release announcing a cornerstone laying ceremony for a housing project named after a prominent New Yorker. You desire to include in this press release some information about this person's contributions to public housing.
   Of the following sources which are available to you, the BEST one to go to in order to obtain this information is

   A. the index and issues of a local newpaper obtainable in the public library
   B. the World Almanac
   C. a book on the history of public housing
   D. a biography of the individual

   1.____

2. You have been assigned to prepare a press release announcing the issuance of applications for apartments at a new city housing project. Of the following items of information, the one which it is LEAST important to include in such a press release is the

   A. average cost per apartment
   B. rental charges per room
   C. number of apartments in the project
   D. special facilities available at the project

   2.____

3. The chairman of the housing authority has asked you to assist him in preparing a speech he is to deliver at the ground-breaking ceremonies for the Authority's 100th permanent housing project. Members of the city, state and federal administrations will be present, as well as the press and the general public.
   Of the following, the theme which you should emphasize *most* in this speech is the

   A. role of the chairman in expediting housing progress
   B. failure of private industry to provide for the housing needs of low-income families
   C. steady march toward the elimination of the city's slums
   D. benefits of living in a democracy

   3.____

4. You have been assigned to prepare an information brochure which is to be distributed to public welfare clients. After preliminary study you find that the value of this brochure will be greatly increased if it is prepared in such a way as to include several pictorial illustrations. You do not have the skill necessary to prepare these illustrations.
   Of the following, the *best* action for you to take is to

   A. prepare the brochure in such a manner as not to require illustrations
   B. ask another employee, who can do the illustrations, to assist you by doing the illustrations
   C. prepare the brochure with such illustrations as you are able to draw
   D. find out first whether someone will be available to do the illustrations for you

   4.____

5. The deputy commissioner of the Department of Welfare has asked you to assist him in preparing a speech. The deputy commissioner is to represent the department as the guest of honor at a banquet given by a civic organization.
Of the following, the *most desirable* action for you to take before beginning to write this speech is to

   A. consult the civic organization to secure background material
   B. arrange for a brief conference with the deputy commissioner in order to determine his wishes as to the general tone and content of the speech
   C. secure a copy of a speech delivered on a similar previous occasion and closely model your speech after it
   D. find out whether the speech will be broadcast

6. Of the following, it is generally *most desirable* that informational material written for reading by public welfare clients be

   A. brief and concise
   B. easily understood
   C. couched in correct technical terms
   D. easy to translate into foreign languages

7. Suppose that you are assigned to release department information to reporters for the metropolitan press. Of the following, the LEAST desirable practice for you to adopt in this assignment is

   A. as a general rule, release information in written form only
   B. set regular dates for the release of department news insofar as possible
   C. secure clearance for the issuance of all written releases
   D. release information first to reporters for newspapers which give the best coverage to department news

8. A letter from a private citizen, complaining about a department policy which has worked a hardship on him, has been referred to you for reply. The citizen asks that this policy be changed.
In answering this letter, it would be *best* to give major emphasis to

   A. an explanation of the reasons which make such a policy necessary
   B. pointing out that the department regulations cannot be revised to suit each individual case
   C. stating that the operations of any large organization must result in some hardships
   D. inducing the individual to come into the office where the matter can better be dealt with in a face-to-face interview

9. Suppose you are assigned to prepare the annual report for your department. Each bureau has been asked to submit a written report on its activities for the preceding year. Of the following, the *most desirable* action for you to take in carrying out this assignment is to

   A. return to the bureau heads for revision those reports which, in your opinion, contain unimportant material
   B. rewrite the material submitted by the bureaus to secure improved style without changing content

C. arrange a conference with the bureau heads to discuss the reports they are to submit
D. write an introduction and conclusion and let the reports of the bureaus constitute, unaltered, the body of the annual report

10. You have been assigned by your supervisor to do the preliminary editing of material written by other information assistants. After a week in this assignment you evaluate the material submitted by one information assistant as of lower quality than that of the others.
Of the following, the *best* action for you to take is to

    A. analyze his work with the other information assistants
    B. continue to edit his work without comment at this time
    C. suggest to him that he take a refresher course in writing
    D. recommend his transfer to less original work

11. You have completed gathering the necessary data for a routine newspaper release you are to write. The *most desirable* step for you to take next is to

    A. write a first draft of the release
    B. work out a plan for the release, including the beginning, the main points, and the ending
    C. develop a suitable title and then begin to write
    D. have someone familiar with the field check the accuracy of the data which you have gathered

12. Of the following writing techniques, the one which is generally LEAST effective for making written matter more forceful is the

    A. repetition of a key word or phrase
    B. liberal use of exclamation points, capitalization, underlining, and other similar devices
    C. use of the verbs in the active voice, rather than the passive voice
    D. use of a brief sentence, rather than a longer one, to express the same idea

13. The use of anecdotes and other verbal illustrations in writing is desirable *primarily* because

    A. this is a good way of showing the author's interest in his subject
    B. the reader will remember the anecdotes
    C. the illustrations will help the reader to remember the author's main idea
    D. the illustrations will entertain the reader

14. The technique of directly addressing the reader of a novel or short story

    A. has been gaining favor steadily during recent years
    B. has been the prevailing practice for a long time
    C. is more common in popular fiction than in literary fiction
    D. is considered out-of-date today

15. The one of the following which is considered LEAST important is good newswriting is 15.____

   A. complete accuracy of names and addresses
   B. full identification of sources of information
   C. strict chronological order of presentation
   D. avoiding the use of editorial statements

16. Of the following, the *best* procedure to follow when writing an article to be read by experts is to 16.____

   A. avoid the technical terms as far as possible
   B. explain the technical terms the first time they are used
   C. use the technical terms of the experts
   D. use your literary judgment as to whether to use the technical terms

17. Of the following, the purpose for which it is LEAST important for a writer to have a large vocabulary is to 17.____

   A. give him a wider choice of synonyms and antonyms
   B. enable him to express himself in a sophisticated language
   C. improve his reading comprehension
   D. make his writing more exact

18. "The family lived in a small edifice on Maple Street." 18.____
    The preceding sentence involves a

   A. good choice of words
   B. poor choice of words because an "edifice" is large rather than small
   C. poor choice of words because the word "edifice" is obsolete
   D. poor choice of words because the word "edifice" is unfamiliar to the average reader

19. In fiction, the *best* way of acquainting the reader with the traits of the characters is through 19.____

   A. action
   B. dialogue and description
   C. action and dialogue
   D. dialogue

20. Subheads in an informal pamphlet 20.____

   A. are a matter of individual preference
   B. are appropriate *only* if the subject readily breaks itself down into separate sections
   C. should be used because the pamphlet will be easier to read
   D. should NOT be used because they look "textbookish"

21. The length of an average paragraph should 21.____

   A. be about 300 words
   B. harmonize with other elements of a writer's style
   C. not fall below 60 words
   D. vary according to each writing assignment

22. In writing for today's readers, the one of the following which would be LEAST suitable as a literary model for imitation is

   A. Abraham Lincoln
   B. Samuel Johnson
   C. Mark Twain
   D. Benjamin Franklin

23. Fictitious characters in factual writing should

   A. be disguised to make them appear real
   B. be given names rather than symbols
   C. be given symbols, such as A, B, and C, rather than names
   D. not be used

24. "Cliches should be avoided in writing." The one of the following which is NOT a cliche is

   A. "every Tom, Dick, and Harry"
   B. "left no stone unturned"
   C. "outrageous possibilities"
   D. "strike while the iron is hot"

25. Recent polls of the general public indicate that from 20% to 80% of the American people are unacquainted with such items of general information as the United Nations and the Marshall plan. Of the following, the *most probable* cause for this lack of knowledge is that

   A. people generally don't read enough to grasp this information
   B. most people don't know anything about current events or international relations
   C. the schools avoid the teaching of controversial subjects
   D. this news was not dealt with in the newspapers read by the people polled

26. The *Readers' Guide to Periodical Literature* is

   A. a digest of magazine articles
   B. a literary magazine
   C. an index of magazine articles
   D. an annual guide to magazine

27. Of the following metropolitan New York newspapers, the one which has the largest daily circulation is the

   A. Daily News
   B. Newsday
   C. New York Times
   D. New York Post

28. The cost-of-living index is computed by the

   A. Bureau of Internal Revenue
   B. Bureau of Labor Statistics
   C. Federal Security Agency
   D. National Bureau of Standards

29. The trend revealed by the U.S. census with regard to the population of metropolitan areas may *best* be described as one of

   A. little change
   B. marked decline
   C. sharp growth
   D. shift from the center to the suburbs

30. In the United States, agreements that prohibit or restrict the sale of real estate to particular racial groups

   A. are a very common legal practice
   B. are commonly practiced in the South
   C. were declared legal and enforceable by the U.S. Supreme Court
   D. were declared legally unenforceable by the U.S. Supreme Court

31. Of the following sentences, the one which is poorly written because it contains a "dangling construction" is

   A. After waiting half an hour for the bus, I remembered that I had no money for carfare.
   B. Having returned from our vacations, the supervisor made reassignments.
   C. Smiling pleasantly, she acknowledged the applause of the audience.
   D. Walking over to him, I introduced myself and offered to help him catch his assailant.

QUESTIONS 32-36.

Questions 32-36 consist of three sentences each. For each question select the sentence which contains NO error in grammar or usage and write the capital letter preceding that sentence in the correspondingly numbered space on your answer sheet.

32. A. Be sure that everybody brings his notes to the conference.
    B. He looked like he meant to hit the boy.
    C. Mr. Jones is one of the clients who was chosen to represent the district.
    D. All are incorrect

33. A. He is taller than I.
    B. I'll have nothing to do with these kind of people.
    C. The reason why he will not buy the house is because it is too expensive.
    D. All are incorrect

34. A. Aren't I eligible for this apartment.
    B. Have you seen him anywheres?
    C. He should of come earlier.
    D. All are incorrect

35. A. He graduated college in 1982.
    B. He hadn't but one more line to write.
    C. Who do you think is the author of this report?
    D. All are incorrect

36. A. I talked to one official, whom I knew was fully impartial.
    B. Everyone signed the petition but him.
    C. He proved not only to be a good student but also a good athlete.
    D. All are incorrect

QUESTIONS 37-40.

Questions 37-40 consist of three sentences each. For each item, select the sentence which contains NO error in word usage and write the capital letter preceding that sentence in the correspondingly numbered space on your answer sheet.

37. A. Every year a large amount of tenants are admitted to housing projects.
    B. Henry Ford owned around a billion dollars in industrial equipment.
    C. He was aggravated by the child's bead behavior.
    D. All are incorrect

37._____

38. A. Before he was committed to the asylum he suffered from the illusion that he was Napoleon.
    B. Besides stocks, there were also bonds in the safe.
    C. We bet the other team easily.
    D. All are incorrect

38._____

39. A. Bring this report to your supervisor immediately.
    B. He set the chair down near the table.
    C. The capitol of New York is Albany.
    D. All are incorrect

39._____

40. A. He was chosen to arbitrate the dispute because every one knew he would be disinterested.
    B. It is advisable to obtain the best council before making an important decision.
    C. Less college students are interested in teaching than ever before.
    D. All are incorrect

40._____

KEY (CORRECT ANSWERS)

1. D	11. B	21. D	31. B
2. A	12. B	22. B	32. A
3. C	13. C	23. B	33. A
4. D	14. D	24. C	34. D
5. B	15. C	25. A	35. C
6. B	16. C	26. C	36. B
7. D	17. B	27. C	37. D
8. A	18. B	28. B	38. B
9. C	19. C	29. D	39. B
10. B	20. C	30. D	40. A

TEST 2

DIRECTIONS: Each question or incomplete statement is followed by several suggested answers or completions. Select the one that BEST answers the question or completes the statement. *PRINT THE LETTER OF THE CORRECT ANSWER IN THE SPACE AT THE RIGHT.*

1. "Study your audience and slant your writing toward it." Of the following, the BEST procedure to adopt in applying this principle is to   1._____

   A. estimate the intelligence of your audience and write accordingly
   B. use the simplest possible prose style
   C. write about the things you believe your audience wants to read, rather than the things you would prefer to write about
   D. write about what you want to say in the form that is most likely to appeal to your audience

2. "The first rule for giving your writing 'punch' is to take the most important idea and save it until the end of the sentence."   2._____
   Of the following sentences, the one which BEST illustrates this principle is:

   A. After they had notified the police, and had searched the entire neighborhood for hours, they found the little girl in the attic, sleeping peacefully.
   B. The enemy has destroyed the lives of our people, plundered our seas, ravaged our coasts, and burnt our towns.
   C. The thief had stolen the top secret report, broken open the safe, and rifled the desk.
   D. The tornado left ruin and death in its wake and tore down every building in the village.

3. "America has been built by the cooperative effort of many different kinds of people, working together."   3._____
   In the preceding sentence, a word or phrase which is NOT made superfluous by the use of another word or phrase of similar meaning is

   A. different   B. kinds of
   C. many   D. working together

4. "The company did so well this year that, at the end of the year, it gave each employee a carton of cigarettes, a bottle of wine, and – a $100 bond."   4._____
   In the preceding sentence, the dash

   A. adds more force to the words which follow
   B. detracts from the force of the words which follow
   C. is an illustration of the improper use of punctuation
   D. neither adds nor detracts from the force of the words which follow

5. A letter written by another information assistant begins with this sentence: "We beg to acknowledge yours of the 23d inst." It then goes on to reply directly to the matters raised in the letter of the 23d.   5._____
   If you are assigned to edit this letter, the most desirable action of the following for you to take is to

A. change the first sentence to read: "We beg to acknowledge yours of the 23d inst. and in reply wish to state that..."
B. leave the first sentence as it is
C. leave the first sentence unchanged but add another immediately following summarizing what the letter of the 23d inquired about
D. omit the first sentence in its entirety

6. "Write as you talk" is an axiom now widely accepted by newspapermen. Newspaper readers have a better chance of grasping the news if it is told to them simply and clearly. The *most direct* implication of the preceding statement is that

    A. an axiom is a statement whose truth is generally accepted by everyone
    B. flowery or complicated language should generally be avoided in newspaper reporting
    C. newspaper readers are no different from newspaper reporters
    D. the use of ungrammatical constructions is sometimes justified in writing for the newspapers

7. "Nowadays, lack of information usually goes hand in hand with little education; similarly, lack of information also usually goes hand in hand with low income. So, if you are writing for people in the lower income brackets or people who haven't gone to college, it's a good guess that they won't have much background knowledge."
The preceding statement implies *most directly* that

    A. little education has always been negatively correlated with little information
    B. poor people are usually not well-informed
    C. people who have not gone to college are in the lower income brackets
    D. writing for the poor and uneducated is more difficult than writing for the rich and well-educated

8. "Prices of building materials are, in the aggregate, more rigid than those of other commodities. Concentration of control over the supply of goods is frequently advanced as the explanation for price rigidities in general and for building materials in particular."
According to the preceding statement,

    A. increased demand and concurrent fixed supply are frequently responsible for increased prices of building materials
    B. in the aggregate, the high cost of building materials contributes substantially to the high cost of new housing construction
    C. the cost of most articles is generally more flexible than the cost of articles required in the construction of new buildings
    D. the existence of faulty methods of distribution is often advanced as an argument to explain price inequities

9. "In undertaking a new development, the builder first decides upon the price or rental range of the dwellings he proposes to construct. Then, after roughly estimating the cost of the selected structure, he tries to find land at suitable prices."
According to the preceding statement,

    A. after a new development is completed, the builder adds up his construction and land costs and fixes the price of the individual house accordingly
    B. it is difficult to predict the probable cost of a new dwelling unit because of constant fluctuation in the cost of building materials

C. land costs influence the selling price of dwellings least
D. the selling price of a house is usually determined before construction is begun

10. "A construction program initiated by public agencies better protects the home buyer and insures the greater soundness of the neighborhood."
According to the preceding statement,

   A. a home buyer is more confident of the safety of his investment if he is given to understand that the neighborhood will not change
   B. a public agency is more responsible in construction programs than a private builder could hope to be
   C. since a public agency can, if necessary, control the development of a neighborhood through zoning laws, public housing is more desirable
   D. to insure the soundness of a neighborhood it is more effective to have the building of new homes planned by public agencies

11. "To achieve sound planning we cannot rely on educating the builder to the fact that what is good for the public will be ultimately good for him, for his interest is usually short term and the pattern in which he functions is not set up for voluntary reform."
According to the preceding statement,

   A. a builder is not interest in educating the public to its ultimate benefits
   B. builders whose interests are usually of short duration can be educated to set up voluntary reforms
   C. since a builder's interest in any property is usually of short duration, he will voluntarily function for public benefit
   D. we cannot rely on educating a builder to the fact that public benefit is to his advantage in the long run

12. "If cities had a long range objective, if they had plans showing the expected line of growth, plans for their future schools and parks, their houses and their locations, their industries and their locations, their future transportation facilities and their utilities, then with the advent of an emergency requiring government spending they could channel the expenditures and step up the program along the lines of the larger long term plans."
According to the preceding statement,

   A. a city wishing to eliminate slums can with proper planning take advantage of an emergency requiring the channeling of expenditures
   B. an emergency requires the channeling of expenditures so that greater efficiency can be shown in planning
   C. cities which have long range plans can make better use of the funds spent by the government during a depression
   D. long range objectives help a city to devise new plans for the development of parks, schools and other public improvements at a considerable saving

13. "Increment or decrement in city income hangs largely upon the maintenance of the values and valuations of real property, upon the quantity of new improvements that go into the city, upon the profitableness of real estate, upon the advent of booms and depressions, and upon the flow of people into or out of the city."
According to the preceding statement,

   A. a boom or a depression has a marked effect on the flow of people into or out of a city

B. new improvements that go into a city enhance the profitableness of real estate
C. real estate values, which form the major basis of a city's taxation, are the sources of city salaries
D. the variation of a city's income depends on the values of the real estate in the city

14. "The institution of the family is a vitally important part of all human societies, but in modern society, particularly, various organized services have developed that enable some people to secure some of the most essential benefits of family life without belonging to a family group."
Of the following, the LEAST valid inference on the basis of the preceding statement is that

    A. people who are not part of a family unit can obtain most of the essential benefits of family life by contacting an appropriate social agency
    B. present day society offers an opportunity to some who are not members of a family unit to share in some of the benefits of family living
    C. the institution of the family is not native to modern society alone
    D. to obtain the benefits of family life it is usually necessary to belong to a family group

15. "Reform organizations seek, as a rule, to bring about a specific economic or political change; social work agencies are usually occupied with the task of meeting existing situations in the lives of particular individuals or groups."
According to the preceding statement,

    A. a reform organization is concerned with helping the individual by changing some factor in the environment which the individual feels is too arduous to accept
    B. a reform organization is not concerned with the ability of the individual to meet his social responsibilities
    C. social work agencies are not concerned with any specific economic or political change because this does not involve the individual's personal adjustment
    D. social workers are primarily concerned with helping their clients to meet current living conditions

16. "Adequate facilities for education, recreation and health must be provided for children, and social conditions created that promote the child's development into a law-abiding citizen. It is not the task of social work to provide these facilities but to direct children to them and to help them to use these facilities."
Of the following, the *most accurate* statement on the basis of the preceding statement is that

    A. a child who does not have adequate educational, recreational and health facilities will develop into a poor citizen
    B. the education of the public to the importance of providing adequate facilities for children is primarily the social worker's responsibility
    C. the proper use of leisure time by children is an important aspect of the social worker's job
    D. the three most important needs of a child which must be satisfied first are those of education, recreation and health

17. "Social workers start from the assumption that preservation: of the family as the basic unit of social living is their accepted objective. In view of the frequency of divorce and the breakdown of authority in the home, social work now makes articulate its concern for family integrity."
According to the preceding statement,

    A. failure to keep the family as a basic unit leads to a breakdown of authority in the home, upsetting family integrity
    B. in extreme cases where divorce is inevitable a social worker must accept the breakdown of the family unit
    C. social workers are primarily concerned with keeping a family together as a basic entity of social living
    D. the importance of the family to society has been demonstrated by experience with children who have been institutionalized

17.____

18. "The marked change in the spirit in which social work is carried on is evidenced in the adoption of business methods of organization, including centralized purchasing of supplies for social agencies, cost accounting, careful budgeting and auditing of accounts, evaluation of methods and publication of reports. Trained personnel for defined jobs is increasingly sought, and there is appreciation of the differentiated abilities required in the social agency."
According to the preceding statement,

    A. it is apparent that the adoption of business methods of organization has resulted in a chage in the method of preparing case work reports
    B. social work agencies that train people for definite jobs achieve savings in social work that approximate those of business organization.
    C. social work now uses current business procedures in carrying forward the pruposes of a social agency
    D. trained personnel in social work are responsible for the adoption of business methods of procedure

18.____

19. "Basic to the functioning of the professional social worker is an understanding of human personality and of the world we live in."
The one of the following which is the *most accurate* statement on the basis of the preceding quotation is that

    A. a social worker must be familiar with human behavior in order to be able to perform his work properly
    B. a social worker who understands human personality is able to function better as a citizen of the world
    C. social work may be classified as a profession because, for its proper performance, a basic understanding of the social and biological sciences is required
    D. through his daily contact with his clients a social worker will obtain a better understanding of the world he lives in

19.____

QUESTIONS 20-24.

Questions 20-24 each consist of three words. For each item, select the word which is INCORRECTLY spelled and write the capital letter preceding that work in the correspondingly numbered space on your answer sheet.

20. A. achievment B. maintenance 20._____
    C. questionnaire D. all are correct

21. A. prevelant B. pronunciation 21._____
    C. separate D. all are correct

22. A. permissible B. relevant 22._____
    C. seize D. all are correct

23. A. corroborate B. desparate 23._____
    C. eighth D. all are correct

24. A. exceed B. feasibility 24._____
    C. psycological D. all are correct

QUESTIONS 25-29.

Use the material which follows in answering questions 25-29.
Copy I on the following page is an accurate copy of material which is to be prepared for the printer. Copy II of this material contains a number of typographical errors. Compare Copy II with Copy I and find the typographical errors. Every group of five lines in Copy II is numbered. Indicate the number of typographical errors in each group of five lines of Copy II by writing in the correspondingly numbered space on the answer sheet the capital letter preceding the best of the following alternatives:

A. no errors B. 1-2 errors
C. 3-4 errors D. 5 or more errors

COPY I

Parcel 1. Beginning at a point formed by the intersection of the northerly side of 73rd avenue with the westerly side of Francis Lewis boulevard as said streets are indicated upon the final map of the borough of Queens known as Alteration Map No. 2831 adopted by the board of estimate on May 15, 1941; running thence northerly along the westerly side of Francis Lewis boulevard following a curve having a radius of 8,053 feet for a distance of 585.15 feet; thence northerly along the westerly side of Francis Lewis boulevard in a straight line for a distance of 687.43 feet; thence northerly along the westerly side of Francis Lewis boulevard and its prolongation following a curve having a radius of 5,677 feet for a distance of 509.79 feet to the old southerly side of North Hempstead turnpike as formerly laid out and as shown discontinued upon the aforementioned final city map; thence easterly along said southerly side of North Hempstead turnpike for 110.12 feet to the easterly side of Francis Lewis boulevard; thence southerly along the easterly side of Francis Lewis boulevard following a curve having a radius of 5.783 feet for a distance of 489.20 feet; thence southerly along the easterly side of Francis Lewis boulevard in a straight line for a distance of 687.43 feet; thence southerly along the easterly side of Francis Lewis boulevard following a curve having a radius of 7,947 feet for a distance of 572.90 feet to the northerly side of 73rd avenue.

COPY II

25. Parcel 1: Beginning at point formed by the intersection of the northerly side of 73rd Avenue with the westerly side of Francis Lewis boulevard as said streets are indicated upon the final map of the borough of Queens known as Alteration Map No. 2831 adapted by the board of estimate on May 15, 1941;

26. running thence northerly along the westerly side of Francis Lewis boulevard following a curve having a radius of 8,053 feet for a distance of 585.15 feet; thence northerly along the westerly side of Francis Lewis boulevard in a straight line for a distance of 687.43 feet; thence northerly along

27. the westerly side of Francis Lewis boulevard and its prolongation following a curve having a radius of 5.677 feet for a distance of 509.79 feet to the old southerly side of North Hempstead Turnpike as formerly laid out and is shown discontinued upon the aforementioned final city map; thence easterly

28. along said southerly side of North Hempstead turnpike for 1101.2 feet to the easterly side of Francis Lewsis boulevard; thence southerly along the easterly side of Francis Lewis boulevard following a curve having a radius of 5.783 feet for a distance of 489.20 feet; thence southerly along the easterly

29. side of Francis Lewis boulevard in a straight line for a distance of 687.43 feet; thence southerly along the easterly side of Francis Lewis boulevard following a curve having a radius of 7,947 feet for a distance of 572.90 feet to the northerly side of 73rd avenue.

30. "He described a hypothetical situation to illustrate his point." In the preceding sentence, the word "hypothetical" means *most nearly*

    A. actual
    B. theoretical
    C. typical
    D. unusual

31. "I gave tacit approval to my partner's proposed business changes." In the preceding sentence, the word "tacit" means *most nearly*

    A. enthusiastic
    B. partial
    C. silent
    D. written

32. "Jones was considered an astute lawyer by the members of his profession." In the preceding sentence, the word "astute" means *most nearly*

    A. clever
    B. persevering
    C. poorly trained
    D. unethical

33. "There were intimations even in early days of the way in which he would go." In the preceding sentence, the word "intimations" means *most nearly*

    A. hints
    B. patterns
    C. plans
    D. purposes

34. "His last book was published posthumously." In the preceding sentence, the word "posthumously" means *most nearly*

    A. after the death of the author
    B. printed free by the publisher
    C. without a dedication
    D. without royalties

35. "When he was challenged, he used every known subterfuge." In the preceding sentence, the word "subterfuge" means *most nearly*

    A. evasion to justify one's conduct
    B. means of attack to defend one's self
    C. medical device
    D. unconscious thought

36. "His partner suggested a course of action that would alleviate the difficulties which confronted him." In the preceding sentence, the word "alleviate" means *most nearly*

    A. correct   B. lessen
    C. remove   D. solve

37. "Among the applicants for the new apartment white collar workers were preponderant." In the preceding sentence, the word "preponderant" means *most nearly*

    A. considered not eligible   B. in evidence
    C. superior in number   D. the first to apply

38. "The captain gave a lucid explanation of his plans for the coming campaign." In the preceding sentence, the word "lucid" means *most nearly*

    A. clear   B. graphic
    C. interesting   D. thorough

39. "He led a sedentary life." In the preceding sentence, the word "sedentary" means *most nearly*

    A. aimless   B. exciting
    C. full   D. inactive

40. "His plan for the next campaign was very plausible." In the preceding sentence, the word "plausible" means *most nearly*

    A. appropriate   B. believable
    C. usable   D. valuable

KEY (CORRECT ANSWERS)

1. D	11. D	21. A	31. C
2. A	12. C	22. D	32. A
3. C	13. D	23. B	33. A
4. A	14. A	24. C	34. A
5. D	15. D	25. C	35. A
6. B	16. C	26. A	36. B
7. B	17. C	27. C	37. C
8. C	18. C	28. B	38. A
9. D	19. A	29. B	39. D
10. D	20. A	30. B	40. B

READING COMPREHENSION
UNDERSTANDING AND INTERPRETING WRITTEN MATERIAL
EXAMINATION SECTION
TEST 1

DIRECTIONS: Each question or incomplete statement is followed by several suggested answers or completions. Select the one that BEST answers the question or completes the statement. *PRINT THE LETTER OF THE CORRECT ANSWER IN THE SPACE AT THE RIGHT.*

Questions 1-4.

DIRECTIONS: Questions 1 through 4 are to be answered SOLELY on the basis of the following paragraph.

    An annual leave allowance, which combines leaves previously given for vacation, personal business, family illness, and other reasons shall be granted members. Calculation of credits for such leave shall be on an annual basis beginning January 1st of each year. Annual leave credits shall be based on time served by members during preceding calendar year. However, when credits have been accrued and member retires during current year, additional annual leave credits shall, in this instance, be granted at accrual rate of three days for each completed month of service, excluding terminal leave. If accruals granted for completed months of service extend into following month, member shall be granted an additional three days accrual for completed month. This shall be the only condition where accruals in a current year are granted for vacation period in such year.

1. According to the above paragraph, if a fireman's wife were to become seriously ill so that he would take time off from work to be with her, such time off would be deducted from his _____ allowance.

    A. annual leave
    B. vacation leave
    C. personal business leave
    D. family illness leave

    1._____

2. Terminal leave means leave taken

    A. at the end of the calendar year
    B. at the end of the vacation year
    C. immediately before retirement
    D. before actually earned, because of an emergency

    2._____

3. A fireman appointed on July 1, 2007 will be able to take his first full or normal annual leave during the period

    A. July 1, 2007 to June 30, 2008
    B. Jan. 1, 2008 to Dec. 31, 2008
    C. July 1, 2008 to June 30, 2009
    D. Jan. 1, 2009 to Dec. 31, 2009

    3._____

4. According to the above paragraph, a member who retires on July 15 of this year will be entitled to receive leave allowance based on this year of _____ days.   4._____

   A. 15   B. 18   C. 22   D. 24

5. Fire alarm boxes are electromechanical devices for transmitting a coded signal. In each box, there is a trainwork of wheels. When the box is operated, a spring-activated code wheel within begins to revolve. The code number of the box is notched on the circumference of the code wheel, and the latter is associated with the circuit in such a way that when it revolves it causes the circuit to open and close in a predetermined manner, thereby transmitting its particular signal to the central station. A fire alarm box is nothing more than a device for interrupting the flow of current in a circuit in such a way as to produce a coded signal that may be decoded by the dispatchers in the central office.
Based on the above, select the FALSE statement: 5._____

   A. Each standard fire alarm box has its own code wheel
   B. The code wheel operates when the box is pulled
   C. The code wheel is operated electrically
   D. Only the break in the circuit by the notched wheel causes the alarm signal to be transmitted to the central office

Questions 6-9.

DIRECTIONS: Questions 6 through 9 are to be answered SOLELY on the basis of the following paragraph.

Ventilation, as used in fire fighting operations, means opening up a building or structure in which a fire is burning to release the accumulated heat, smoke, and gases. Lack of knowledge of the principles of ventilation on the part of firemen may result in unnecessary punishment due to ventilation being neglected or improperly handled. While ventilation itself extinguishes no fires, when used in an intelligent manner, it allows firemen to get at the fire more quickly, easily, and with less danger and hardship.

6. According to the above paragraph, the MOST important result of failure to apply the principles of ventilation at a fire may be   6._____

   A. loss of public confidence
   B. waste of water
   C. excessive use of equipment
   D. injury to firemen

7. It may be inferred from the above paragraph that the CHIEF advantage of ventilation is that it   7._____

   A. eliminates the need for gas masks
   B. reduces smoke damage
   C. permits firemen to work closer to the fire
   D. cools the fire

8. Knowledge of the principles of ventilation, as defined in the above paragraph, would be LEAST important in a fire in a   8._____

   A. tenement house
   B. grocery store
   C. ship's hold
   D. lumberyard

9. We may conclude from the above paragraph that for the well-trained and equipped fireman, ventilation is   9._____

   A. a simple matter
   B. rarely necessary
   C. relatively unimportant
   D. a basic tool

Questions 10-13.

DIRECTIONS: Questions 10 through 13 are to be answered SOLELY on the basis of the following passage.

Fire exit drills should be established and held periodically to effectively train personnel to leave their working area promptly upon proper signal and to evacuate the building, speedily but without confusion. All fire exit drills should be carefully planned and carried out in a serious manner under rigid discipline so as to provide positive protection in the event of a real emergency. As a general rule, the local fire department should be furnished advance information regarding the exact date and time the exit drill is scheduled. When it is impossible to hold regular drills, written instructions should be distributed to all employees.

Depending upon individual circumstances, fires in warehouses vary from those of fast development that are almost instantly beyond any possibility of employee control to others of relatively slow development where a small readily attackable flame may be present for periods of time up to 15 minutes or more during which simple attack with fire extinguishers or small building hoses may prevent the fire development. In any case, it is characteristic of many warehouse fires that at a certain point in development they flash up to the top of the stack, increase heat quickly, and spread rapidly. There is a degree of inherent danger in attacking warehouse type fires, and all employees should be thoroughly trained in the use of the types of extinguishers or small hoses in the buildings and well instructed in the necessity of always staying between the fire and a direct pass to an exit.

10. Employees should be instructed that, when fighting a fire, they MUST   10._____

    A. try to control the blaze
    B. extinguish any fire in 15 minutes
    C. remain between the fire and a direct passage to the exit
    D. keep the fire between themselves and the fire exit

11. Whenever conditions are such that regular fire drills cannot be held, then which one of the following actions should be taken?   11._____

    A. The local fire department should be notified.
    B. Rigid discipline should be maintained during work hours.
    C. Personnel should be instructed to leave their working area by whatever means are available.
    D. Employees should receive fire drill procedures in writing.

12. The above passage indicates that the purpose of fire exit drills is to train employees to   12._____

    A. control a fire before it becomes uncontrollable
    B. act as firefighters
    C. leave the working area promptly
    D. be serious

13. According to the above passage, fire exit drills will prove to be of UTMOST effectiveness   13._____
    if

    A. employee participation is made voluntary
    B. they take place periodically
    C. the fire department actively participates
    D. they are held without advance planning

Questions 14-16.

DIRECTIONS: Questions 14 through 16 are to be answered SOLELY on the basis of the following paragraph.

The heat output from unit heaters will depend on how fast and how completely dry hot steam fills the unit core. For complete and fast air removal and rapid drainage of condensate, use a trap actuated by water or vapor (inverted bucket trap) and not a trap operated by temperature only (thermostatic or bellows trap). A temperature-actuated trap will hold back the hot condensate until it cools to a point where the thermal element opens. When this happens, the condensate backs up in the heater and reduces the heat output. With a water-actuated trap, this will not happen as the water or condensate is discharged as fast as it is formed.

14. On the basis of the information given in the above paragraph, it can be concluded that   14._____
    the PROPER type of trap to use for a unit heater is a(n) _____ trap.

    A. thermostatic   B. bellows-type
    C. inverted bucket   D. temperature

15. According to the above paragraph, the MAIN reason for using the type of trap specified   15._____
    for a unit heater is to

    A. bring the condensate up to steam temperature
    B. prevent reduction in the heat output of the unit heater
    C. permit cycling of the heater
    D. maintain constant temperature of condensate in the trap

16. As used in the above paragraph, the word *actuated* means MOST NEARLY   16._____

    A. clogged   B. operated   C. cleaned   D. vented

Question 17 -25.

DIRECTIONS: Questions 17 through 25 are to be answered SOLELY on the basis of the following passage. Each question consists of a statement. You are to indicate whether the statement is TRUE (T) or FALSE (F).

MOVING AN OFFICE

An office with all its equipment is sometimes moved during working hours. This is a difficult task and must be done in an orderly manner to avoid confusion. The operation should be planned in such a way as not to interrupt the progress of work usually done in the office and to make possible the accurate placement of the furniture and records in the new location. If the office moves to a place inside the same building, the desks and files are moved with all their contents. If the movement is to another building, the contents of each desk and file are placed in boxes. Each box is marked with a letter showing the particular section in the new quarters to which it is to be moved. Also marked on each box is the number of the desk or file on which the box is to be placed. Each piece of equipment must have a numbered tag. The number of each piece of equipment is put in soft chalk on the floor in the new office to show the proper location, and several floor plans are made to show where each piece of equipment goes. When the moving is done, someone is stationed at each of the several exits of the old office to see that each box or piece of equipment has its destination clearly marked on it. At the new office, someone stands at each of the several entrances with a copy of the floor plan and directs the placing of the furniture and equipment according to the floor plan. No one should interfere at this point with the arrangements shown on the plan. Improvements in arrangement can be considered and made at a later date.

17. It is a hard job to move an office from one place to another during working hours. 17.____

18. Confusion cannot be avoided if an office is moved during working hours. 18.____

19. The work usually done in an office must be stopped for the day when the office is moved during working hours. 19.____

20. If an office is moved from one floor to another in the same building, the contents of a desk are taken out and put into boxes for moving. 20.____

21. If boxes are used to hold material from desks when moving an office, the box is numbered the same as the desk on which it is to be put. 21.____

22. Letters are marked in soft chalk on the floor at the new quarters to show where the desks should go when moved. 22.____

23. When the moving begins, a person is put at each exit of the old office to check that each box and piece of equipment has clearly marked on it where it to go. 23.____

24. A person stationed at each entrance of the new quarters to direct the placing of the furniture and equipment has a copy of the floor plan of the new quarters. 24.____

25. If, while the furniture is being moved into the new office, a person helping at a doorway gets an idea of a better way to arrange the furniture, he should change the planned arrangement and make a record of the change. 25.____

KEY (CORRECT ANSWERS)

1.	A	11.	D
2.	C	12.	C
3.	D	13.	B
4.	B	14.	C
5.	C	15.	B
6.	D	16.	B
7.	C	17.	T
8.	D	18.	F
9.	D	19.	F
10.	C	20.	F

21. T
22. F
23. T
24. T
25. F

———

TEST 2

Questions 1-4.

DIRECTIONS: Questions 1 through 4 are to be answered SOLELY on the basis of the following paragraph.

In all cases of homicide, members of the Police Department who investigate will make every effort to obtain statements from dying persons. Such statements are of the greatest importance to the District Attorney. In many cases, there may be a failure to solve the crime if they are not taken. The principal element to be considered in taking the declaration of a dying person is his mental attitude. In order to be admissible in evidence, the person must have no hope of recovery. The patient will be fully interrogated on that point before a statement is taken.

1. In cases of homicide, according to the above paragraph, members of the police force will

    A. try to change the mental attitude of the dying person
    B. attempt to obtain a statement from the dying person
    C. not give the information they obtain directly to the District Attorney
    D. be careful not to injure the dying person unnecessarily

1.____

2. The mental attitude of the person making the dying statement is of GREAT importance because it can determine, according to the above paragraph, whether the

    A. victim should be interrogated in the presence of witnesses
    B. victim will be willing to make a statement of any kind
    C. statement will tell the District Attorney who committed the crime
    D. the statement can be used as evidence

2.____

3. District Attorneys find that statements of a dying person are important, according to the above paragraph, because

    A. it may be that the victim will recover and then refuse to testify
    B. they are important elements in determining the mental attitude of the victim
    C. they present a point of view
    D. it may be impossible to punish the criminal without such a statement

3.____

4. A well-known gangster is found dying from a bullet wound. The patrolman first on the scene, in the presence of witnesses, tells the man that he is going to die and asks, *Who shot you?* The gangster says, *Jones shot me, but he hasn't killed me. I'll live to get him.* He then falls back dead. According to the above paragraph, this statement is

    A. *admissible* in evidence; the man was obviously speaking the truth
    B. *not admissible* in evidence; the man obviously did not believe that he was dying
    C. *admissible* in evidence; there were witnesses to the statement
    D. *not admissible* in evidence; the victim did not sign any statement and the evidence is merely hearsay

4.____

Questions 5-7.

DIRECTIONS: Questions 5 through 7 are to be answered SOLELY on the basis of the following paragraph.

The factors contributing to crime and delinquency are varied and complex. The home and its immediate environment have been found to be crucial in determining the behavior patterns of the individual, and criminality can frequently be traced to faulty family relationships and a bad neighborhood. But in the search for a clearer understanding of the underlying causes of delinquent and criminal behavior, the total environment must be taken into consideration.

5. According to the above paragraph, family relationships 5._____

   A. tend to become faulty in bad neighborhoods
   B. are important in determining the actions of honest people as well as criminals
   C. are the only important element in the understanding of causes of delinquency
   D. are determined by the total environment

6. According to the above paragraph, the causes of crime and delinquency are 6._____

   A. not simple   B. not meaningless
   C. meaningless   D. simple

7. According to the above paragraph, faulty family relationships FREQUENTLY are 7._____

   A. responsible for varied and complex results
   B. caused when one or both parents have a criminal behavior pattern
   C. independent of the total environment
   D. the cause of criminal acts

Questions 8-10.

DIRECTIONS: Questions 8 through 10 are to be answered SOLELY on the basis of the following paragraph.

A change in the specific problems which confront the police and in the methods for dealing with them has taken place in the last few decades. The automobile is a two-way symbol of this change in policing. It menaces every city with a complicated traffic problem and has speeded up the process of committing a crime and making a getaway, but at the same time has increased the effectiveness of police operations. However, the major concern of police departments continues to be the antisocial or criminal actions and behavior of human beings.

8. On the basis of the above paragraph, it can be stated that, for the most part, in the past few decades the specific problems of a police force 8._____

   A. have changed but the general problems have not
   B. as well as the general problems have changed
   C. have remained the same but the general problems have changed
   D. as well as the general problems have remained the same

9. According to the above paragraph, advances in science and industry have, in general, made the police 9._____

   A. operations less effective from the overall point of view
   B. operations more effective from the overall point of view
   C. abandon older methods of solving police problems
   D. concern themselves more with the antisocial acts of human beings

10. The automobile is a *two-way symbol,* according to the above paragraph, because its use   10._____

    A. has speeded up getting to and away from the scene of a crime
    B. both helps and hurts police operations
    C. introduces a new antisocial act—traffic violation—and does away with criminals like horse thieves
    D. both increases and decreases speed by introducing traffic problems

Questions 11-14.

DIRECTIONS: Questions 11 through 14 are to be answered SOLELY on the basis of the following passage on INSTRUCTIONS TO COIN AND TOKEN CASHIERS.

INSTRUCTIONS TO COIN AND TOKEN CASHIERS

Cashiers should reset the machine registers to an even starting number before commencing the day's work. Money bags received directly from collecting agents shall be counted and receipted for on the collecting agent's form. Each cashier shall be responsible for all coin or token bags accepted by him. He must examine all bags to be used for bank deposits for cuts and holes before placing them in use. Care must be exercised so that bags are not cut in opening them. Each bag must be opened separately and verified before another bag is opened. The machine register must be cleared before starting the count of another bag. The amount shown on the machine register must be compared with the amount on the bag tag. The empty bag must be kept on the table for re-examination should there be a difference between the amount on the bag tag and the amount on the machine register.

11. A cashier should BEGIN his day's assignment by   11._____

    A. counting and accepting all money bags
    B. resetting the counting machine register
    C. examining all bags for cuts and holes
    D. verifying the contents of all money bags

12. In verifying the amount of money in the bags received from the collecting agent, it is BEST to   12._____

    A. check the amount in one bag at a time
    B. base the total on the amount on the collecting agent's form
    C. repeat the total shown on the bag tag
    D. refer to the bank deposit receipt

13. A cashier is instructed to keep each empty coin bag on his table while verifying its contents CHIEFLY because, long as the bag is on the table,   13._____

    A. it cannot be misplaced
    B. the supervisor can see how quickly the cashier works
    C. cuts and holes are easily noticed
    D. a recheck is possible in case the machine count disagrees with the bag tag total

14. The INSTRUCTIONS indicate that it is NOT proper procedure for a cashier to

   A. assume that coin bags are free of cuts and holes
   B. compare the machine register total with the total shown on the bag tag
   C. sign a form when he receives coin bags
   D. reset the machine register before starting the day's counting

Questions 15-17.

DIRECTIONS: Questions 15 through 17 are to be answered SOLELY on the basis of the following passage.

The mass media are an integral part of the daily life of virtually every American. Among these media the youngest, television, is the most pervasive. Ninety-five percent of American homes have at least one T.V. set, and on the average that set is in use for about 40 hours each week. The central place of television in American life makes this medium the focal point of a growing national concern over the effects of media portrayals of violence on the values, attitudes, and behavior of an ever increasing audience.

In our concern about violence and its causes, it is easy to make television a scapegoat. But we emphasize the fact that there is no simple answer to the problem of violence – no single explanation of its causes, and no single prescription for its control. It should be remembered that America also experienced high levels of crime and violence in periods before the advent of television.

The problem of balance, taste, and artistic merit in entertaining programs on television are complex. We cannot <u>countenance</u> government censorship of television. Nor would we seek to impose arbitrary limitations on programming which might jeopardize television's ability to deal in dramatic presentations with controversial social issues. Nonetheless, we are deeply troubled by television's constant portrayal of violence, not in any genuine attempt to focus artistic expression on the human condition, but rather in pandering to a public preoccupation with violence that television itself has helped to generate.

15. According to the above passage, television uses violence MAINLY

   A. to highlight the reality of everyday existence
   B. to satisfy the audience's hunger for destructive action
   C. to shape the values and attitudes of the public
   D. when it films documentaries concerning human conflict

16. Which one of the following statements is BEST supported by the above passage?

   A. Early American history reveals a crime pattern which is not related to television.
   B. Programs should give presentations of social issues and never portray violent acts.
   C. Television has proven that entertainment programs can easily make the balance between taste and artistic merit a simple matter.
   D. Values and behavior should be regulated by governmental censorship.

17. Of the following, which word has the same meaning as *countenance,* as used in the above passage?

   A. Approve   B. Exhibit   C. Oppose   D. Reject

DIRECTIONS: Questions 18 through 21 are to be answered SOLELY on the basis of the following passage.

Maintenance of leased or licensed areas on public parks or lands has always been a problem. A good rule to follow in the administration and maintenance of such areas is to limit the responsibility of any lessee or licensee to the maintenance of the structures and grounds essential to the efficient operation of the concession, not including areas for the general use of the public, such as picnic areas, public comfort stations, etc.; except where such facilities are leased to another public agency or where special conditions make such inclusion practicable, and where a good standard of maintenance can be assured and enforced. If local conditions and requirements are such that public use areas are included, adequate safeguards to the public should be written into contracts and enforced in their administration, to insure that maintenance by the concessionaire shall be equal to the maintenance standards for other park property.

18. According to the above passage, when an area on a public park is leased to a concessionaire, it is usually BEST to

    A. confine the responsibility of the concessionaire to operation of the facilities and leave the maintenance function to the park agency
    B. exclude areas of general public use from the maintenance obligation of the concessionaire
    C. make the concessionaire responsible for maintenance of the entire area including areas of general public use
    D. provide additional comfort station facilities for the area

19. According to the above passage, a valid reason for giving a concessionaire responsibility for maintenance of a picnic area within his leased area is that

    A. local conditions and requirements make it practicable
    B. more than half of the picnic area falls within his leased area
    C. the concessionaire has leased picnic facilities to another public agency
    D. the picnic area falls entirely within his leased area

20. According to the above passage, a precaution that should be taken when a concessionaire is made responsible for maintenance of an area of general public use in a park is

    A. making sure that another public agency has not previously been made responsible for this area
    B. providing the concessionaire with up-to-date equipment, if practicable
    C. requiring that the concessionaire take out adequate insurance for the protection of the public
    D. writing safeguards to the public into the contract

KEY (CORRECT ANSWERS)

1.	B	11.	B
2.	D	12.	A
3.	D	13.	D
4.	B	14.	A
5.	B	15.	B
6.	A	16.	A
7.	D	17.	A
8.	A	18.	B
9.	B	19.	A
10.	B	20.	D

TEST 3

Questions 1-5.

DIRECTIONS: Questions 1 through 5 are to be answered SOLELY on the basis of the following paragraph.

Physical inspections are an important tool for the examiner because he will have to decide the case in many instances on the basis of the inspection report. Most proceedings in a rent office are commenced by the filing of a written application or complaint by an interested party; that is, either the landlord or the tenant. Such an application or complaint must be filed in duplicate in order that the opposing party may be served with a copy of the application or complaint and thus be given an opportunity to answer and oppose it. Sometimes, a further opportunity is given the applicant to file a written rebuttal or reply to his adversary's answer. Often an examiner can make a determination or decision based on the written application, the answer, and the reply to the answer; and, of course, it would speed up operations if it were always possible to make decisions based on written documents only. Unfortunately, decisions can't always be made that way. There are numerous occasions where <u>disputed</u> issues of fact remain which cannot be <u>resolved</u> on the basis of the written statements of the parties. Typical examples are the following: The tenant claims that the refrigerator or stove or bathroom fixture is not functioning properly and the landlord denies this. It is obvious that in such cases an inspection of the accommodations is almost the only means of resolving such disputed issues.

1. According to the above paragraph,

   A. physical inspections are made in all cases
   B. physical inspections are seldom made
   C. it is sometimes possible to determine the facts in a case without a physical inspection
   D. physical inspections are made when it is necessary to verify the examiner's determination

2. According to the above paragraph, in MOST cases, proceedings are started by a(n)

   A. inspector discovering a violation
   B. oral complaint by a tenant or landlord
   C. request from another agency, such as the Building Department
   D. written complaint by a tenant or landlord

3. According to the above paragraph, when a tenant files an application with the rent office, the landlord is

   A. not told about the proceeding until after the examiner makes his determination
   B. given the duplicate copy of the application
   C. notified by means of an inspector visiting the premises
   D. not told about the proceeding until after the inspector has visited the Premises

4. As used in the above paragraph, the word *disputed* means MOST NEARLY

   A. unsettled   B. contested
   C. definite   D. difficult

5. As used in the above paragraph, the word *resolved* means MOST NEARLY 5.____

   A. settled   B. fixed   C. helped   D. amended

Questions 6-10.

DIRECTIONS: Questions 6 through 10 are to be answered SOLELY on the basis of the following paragraph.

   The examiner should order or request an inspection of the housing accommodations. His request for a physical inspection should be in writing, identify the accommodations and the landlord and the tenant, and specify precisely just what the inspector is to look for and report on. Unless this request is specific and lists in detail every item which the examiner wishes to be reported, the examiner will find that the inspection has not served its purpose and that even with the inspector's report, he is still in no position to decide the case due to loose ends which have not been completely tied up. The items that the examiner is interested in should be separately numbered on the inspection request and the same number referred to in the inspector's report. You can see what it would mean if an inspector came back with a report that did not cover everything. It may mean a tremendous waste of time and often require a re-inspection.

6. According to the above paragraph, the inspector makes an inspection on the order of 6.____

   A. the landlord
   B. the tenant
   C. the examiner
   D. both the landlord and the tenant

7. According to the above paragraph, the reason for numbering each item that an inspector reports on is so that 7.____

   A. the report is neat
   B. the report can be easily read and referred to
   C. none of the examiner's requests for information is missed
   D. the report will be specific

8. The one of the following items that is NOT necessarily included in the request for inspection is 8.____

   A. location of dwelling   B. name of landlord
   C. item to be checked   D. type of building

9. As used in the above paragraph, the word precisely means MOST NEARLY 9.____

   A. exactly   B. generally   C. Usually   D. strongly

10. As used in the above paragraph, the words in detail mean MOST NEARLY 10.____

    A. clearly   B. item by item
    C. substantially   D. completely

Questions 11-13.

DIRECTIONS: Questions 11 through 13 are to be answered SOLELY on the basis of the following passage.

The agreement under which a tenant rents property from a landlord is known as a lease. Generally speaking, leases are classified as either short-term or long-term in duration. They are further subdivided according to the method used to determine the amount of periodic rent payments. Of the following types of lease in use, the more commonly used ones are the following:

1. The straight or fixed lease is one in which rent may be paid in equal amounts throughout the duration of the lease. These are usually restricted to short-term leasing, or somewhat longer-term if clauses in the lease provide for periodic escalation of payments as the economy shifts.
2. Percentage leasing, used for short-term commercial leasing, provides the landlord with a stipulated percentage of a tenant's gross sales from goods and services sold on the premises, in addition to a fixed amount of rent.
3. The net lease, generally long-term (ten years or more), requires the tenant to pay all operating costs, including real estate taxes and insurance. In a net-net lease, the tenant further agrees to meet mortgage interest and principal payments.
4. An escalated lease, which is a long-term lease, requires rent to be of a stipulated base amount which periodically is subject to escalation in accordance with cost-of-living index scales, or in direct proportion to taxes, insurance, and operating costs.

11. Based on the information given in the passage, which type of lease is MOST likely to be advantageous to a landlord if there is a high rate of inflation? _____ lease. 11._____

    A. Fixed   B. Percentage   C. Net   D. Escalated

12. On the basis of the above passage, which types of lease would generally be MOST suitable for a well-established textile company which requires permanent facilities for its large operations? 12._____
    _____ lease and _____ lease.

    A. Percentage; escalated   B. Escalated; net
    C. Straight; net   D. Straight; percentage

13. According to the above passage, the ONLY type of lease which assures the same amount of rent throughout a specified interval is the _____ lease. 13._____

    A. straight   B. percentage   C. net-net   D. escalated

Questions 14-15.

DIRECTIONS: Questions 14 and 15 are to be answered SOLELY on the basis of the following passage.

If you like people, if you seek contact with them rather than hide yourself in a corner, if you study your fellow men sympathetically, if you try consistently to contribute something to their success and happiness, if you are reasonably generous with your thought and your time, if you have a partial reserve with everyone but a seeming reserve with no one, you will get along with your superiors, your subordinates, and the human race.

By the scores of thousands, precepts and platitudes have been written for the guidance of personal conduct. The odd part of it is that, despite all of this labor, most of the frictions in modern society arise from the individual's feeling of inferiority, his false pride, his vanity, his unwillingness to yield space to any other man and his consequent urge to throw his own weight around. Goethe said that the quality which best enables a man to renew his own life, in his relation to others, is his capability of renouncing particular things at the right moment in order warmly to embrace something new in the next.

14. On the basis of the above passage, it may be INFERRED that

   A. a person should be unwilling to renounce privileges
   B. a person should realize that loss of a desirable job assignment may come at an opportune moment
   C. it is advisable for a person to maintain a considerable amount of reserve in his relationship with unfamiliar people
   D. people should be ready to contribute generously to a worthy charity

15. Of the following, the MOST valid implication made by the above passage is that

   A. a wealthy person who spends a considerable amount of money entertaining his friends is not really getting along with them
   B. if a person studies his fellow men carefully and impartially, he will tend to have good relationships with them
   C. individuals who maintain seemingly little reserve in their relationships with people have in some measure overcome their own feelings of inferiority
   D. most precepts that have been written for the guidance of personal conduct in relationships with other people are invalid

Questions 16-17.

DIRECTIONS: Questions 16 and 17 are to be answered SOLELY on the basis of the following passage.

When a design for a new bank note of the Federal Government has been prepared by the Bureau of Engraving and Printing and has been approved by the Secretary of the Treasury, the engravers begin the work of cutting the design in steel. No one engraver does all the work. Each man is a specialist. One works only on portraits, another on lettering, another on scroll work, and so on. Each engraver, with a steel tool known as a graver, and aided by a powerful magnifying glass, carefully carves his portion of the design into the steel. He knows that one false cut or a slip of his tool, or one miscalculation of width or depth of line, may destroy the merit of his work. A single mistake means that months or weeks of labor will have been in vain. The Bureau is proud of the fact that no counterfeiter ever has duplicated the excellent work of its expert engravers.

16. According to the above passage, each engraver in the Bureau of Engraving and Printing

   A. must be approved by the Secretary of the Treasury before he can begin work on the design for a new bank note
   B. is responsible for engraving a complete design of a new bank note by himself
   C. designs new bank notes and submits them for approval to the Secretary of the Treasury
   D. performs only a specific part of the work of engraving a design for a new bank note

17. According to the above passage,

    A. an engraver's tools are not available to a counterfeiter
    B. mistakes made in engraving a design can be corrected immediately with little delay in the work of the Bureau
    C. the skilled work of the engravers has not been successfully reproduced by counterfeiter
    D. careful carving and cutting by the engravers is essential to prevent damage to equipment

Questions 18-21.

DIRECTIONS: Questions 18 through 21 are to be answered SOLELY on the basis of the following passage.

In the late fifties, the average American housewife spent $4.50 per day for a family of four on food and 5.15 hours in food preparation, if all of her food was *home prepared;* she spent $5.80 per day and 3.25 hours if all of her food was purchased *partially prepared;* and $6.70 per day and 1.65 hours if all of her food was purchased *ready to serve.*

Americans spent about 20 billion dollars for food products in 1941. They spent nearly 70 billion dollars in 1958. They spent 25 percent of their cash income on food in 1958. For the same kinds and quantities of food that consumers bought in 1941, they would have spent only 16% of their cash income in 1958. It is obvious that our food does cost more. Many factors contribute to this increase besides the additional cost that might be attributed to processing. Consumption of more expensive food items, higher marketing margins, and more food eaten in restaurants are other factors.

The Census of Manufacturers gives some indication of the total bill for processing. The value added by manufacturing of food and kindred products amounted to 3.5 billion of the 20 billion dollars spent for food in 1941. In the year 1958, the comparable figure had climbed to 14 billion dollars.

18. According to the above passage, the cash income of Americans in 1958 was MOST NEARLY _____ billion dollars.

    A. 11.2   B. 17.5   C. 70   D. 280

19. According to the above passage, if Americans bought the same kinds and quantities of food in 1958 as they did in 1941, they would have spent MOST NEARLY _____ billion dollars.

    A. 20   B. 45   C. 74   D. 84

20. According to the above passage, the percent increase in money spent for food in 1958 over 1941, as compared with the percentage increase in money spent for food processing in the same years,

    A. was greater
    B. was less
    C. was the same
    D. cannot be determined from the passage

21. In 1958, an American housewife who bought all of her food ready-to-serve saved in time, as compared with the housewife who prepared all of her food at home

   A. 1.6 hours daily
   B. 1.9 hours daily
   C. 3.5 hours daily
   D. an amount of time which cannot be determined from the above passage

Questions 22-25.

DIRECTIONS: Questions 22 through 25 are to be answered SOLELY on the basis of the following passage.

Any member of the retirement system who is in city service, who files a proper application for service credit and agrees to deductions from his compensation at triple his normal rate of contribution, shall be credited with a period of city service previous to the beginning of his present membership in the retirement system. The period of service credited shall be equal to the period throughout which such triple deductions are made, but may not exceed the total of the city service the member rendered between his first day of eligibility for membership in the retirement system and the day he last became a member. After triple contributions for all of the first three years of service credit claimed, the remaining service credit may be purchased by a single payment of the sum of the remaining payments. If the total time purchasable exceeds ten years, triple contributions may be made for one-half of such time, and the remaining time purchased by a single payment of the sum of the remaining payments. Credit for service acquired in the above manner may be used only in determining the amount of any retirement benefit. Eligibility for such benefit will, in all cases, be based upon service rendered after the employee's membership last began, and will be exclusive of service credit purchased as described below.

22. According to the above passage, in order to obtain credit for city service previous to the beginning of an employee's present membership in the retirement system, the employee must

   A. apply for the service credit and consent to additional contributions to the retirement system
   B. apply for the service credit before he renews his membership in the retirement system
   C. have previous city service which does not exceed ten years
   D. make contributions to the retirement system for three years

23. According to the information in the above passage, credit for city service previous to the beginning of an employee's present membership in the retirement system, is

   A. credited up to a maximum of ten years
   B. credited to any member of the retirement system
   C. used in determining the amount of the employee's benefits
   D. used in establishing the employee's eligibility to receive benefits

24. According to the information in the above passage, a member of the retirement system may purchase service credit for

   A. the period of time between his first day of eligibility for membership in the retirement system and the date he applies for the service credit
   B. one-half of the total of his previous city service if the total time exceeds ten years
   C. the period of time throughout which triple deductions are made
   D. the period of city service between his first day of eligibility for membership in the retirement system and the day he last became a member

25. Suppose that a member of the retirement system has filed an application for service credit for five years of previous city service.
Based on the information in the above passage, the employee may purchase credit for this previous city service by making

   A. triple contributions for three years
   B. triple contributions for one-half of the time and a single payment of the sum of the remaining payments
   C. triple contributions for three years and a single payment of the sum of the remaining payments
   D. a single payment of the sum of the payments

KEY (CORRECT ANSWERS)

1. C	11. D
2. D	12. B
3. B	13. A
4. B	14. B
5. A	15. C
6. C	16. D
7. C	17. C
8. D	18. D
9. A	19. B
10. B	20. B

21. C
22. A
23. C
24. D
25. C

ENGLISH EXPRESSION
CHANGE IN CONSTRUCTION

COMMENTARY

A searching type of multiple-choice question requires the candidate to revise a sentence according to the directions provided for that sentence and choose the word or phrase that will appear in the best revision.

Fundamentally, this question attempts to measure the candidate's ability to re-write or to manipulate a sentence or statement with grammatical correctness, felicity of expression, flexibility in construction, and facility of substitution.

This is actually a subtle method of employing the multiple-choice question to achieve the evaluations ordinarily directly obtained through the traditional essay-writing question.

SAMPLE QUESTIONS

DIRECTIONS: In questions 1 and 2, you are given a complete sentence which you are to rewrite in your mind, starting with the words given just below it.

Make whatever changes the new sentence plan requires, but no others; do not change the overall meaning of the sentence.

Note that you are not correcting a mistake in the original sentence; you are simply changing the construction. The revised sentence should be grammatically correct, but it need not necessarily be a better way of expressing the meaning.

There may be more than one way of recasting the sentence but only one will enable you to answer the question.

Read the directions for each question carefully. They may specify that the missing word or expression appear somewhere in the rewritten sentence; they may ask for the next word in the rewritten sentence, the word following a specific word, etc.

1. Most people acquire about 75 percent of what they learn through the sense of sight.
   REWRITTEN: About 75 percent ....
   Somewhere in the part of the rewritten sentence indicated by dots is the word

   A. them   B. acquired   C. a   D. learning   E. study

   ACCEPTABLY REWRITTEN, the above sentence would read:
   About 75 percent of what most people learn is acquired through the sense of sight.
   You would, therefore, mark B on your answer sheet.

2. Various studies show that a great amount of the absenteeism in factories is caused by preventable accidents.
   REWRITTEN: According to various studies, preventable accidents ...
   The NEXT WORDS in the rewritten sentence are

   A. result from   B. could be   C. are caused by
   D. are related to   E. account for

   ACCEPTABLY REWRITTEN, the above sentence would read:
   According to various studies, preventable accidents account for the great amount of absenteeism in factories.
   You would, therefore, mark E on your answer sheet.

EXAMINATION SECTION
TEST 1

DIRECTIONS: In the following questions, you are given a complete sentence which you are to rewrite in your mind, starting with the words given just below it. Make whatever changes the new sentence plan requires, but no others; do not change the overall meaning of the sentence.

Note that you are not correcting a mistake in the original sentence; you are simply changing the construction. The revised sentence should be grammatically correct, but it need not necessarily be a better way of expressing the meaning. There may be more than one way of recasting the sentence but only one will enable you to answer the question.

Read the directions for each question carefully. They may specify that the missing word or expression appear somewhere in the rewritten sentence; they may ask for the next word in the rewritten sentence, the word following a specific word, etc.

1. As a literary genre, the messianic drama falls into the category of myth or romance, for its central figure conforms to the definitions supplied by Northrup Frye, in THE ANATOMY OF CRITICISM, of the mythic hero.
   REWRITTEN:
   Because its central figure conforms to the definitions of the mythic hero supplied by Northrup Frye, in THE ANATOMY OF CRITICISM, the messianic drama is ....
   The NEXT word in the rewritten sentence is

   A. into B. literary C. categorized
   D. categorically E. a

2. In THE EMPEROR JULIAN, the second part of the drama, Ibsen reveals Julian to be a false Messiah.
   REWRITTEN:
   Julian is .....
   Somewhere in the part of the rewritten sentence indicated by dots is the word

   A. reveals B. by C. falsified
   D. in which E. messianic

3. More interesting, because more subtly hidden, is Chekhov's use of melodrama.
   REWRITTEN:
   Because it is more .....
   The NEXT word in the rewritten sentence is

   A. subtly B. interesting C. melodramatic
   D. used E. hidden

4. Shaw's response to this is to withdraw, partially, from his public concerns into a more personal, private, and poetic form of expression.
   REWRITTEN:
   Shaw responded to this with a .... .
   Somewhere in the part of the rewritten sentence indicated by dots is the word

   A. partially B. is to C. withdraws
   D. publicly E. withdrawal

5. D
6. A
7. B
8. C
9. E
10. A

11. To have the program succeed, Marx realized he would need the united support of workingmen all over the world.
    REWRITTEN:
    Marx realized that the success .....
    Somewhere in the part of the rewritten sentence indicated by dots is the word

    A. he B. would C. have
    D. required E. to

12. His beautiful descriptions of nature reflect the poet's deep belief in the closeness of nature to the human soul.
    REWRITTEN:
    One reflection of .....
    The NEXT word(s) in the rewritten sentence is(are)

    A. beauty B. the poet's C. poetry
    D. the descriptions E. closeness

13. The extraordinary play is a chronicle of O'Neill's own spiritual metamorphosis from a messianic into an existential rebel.
    REWRITTEN:
    O'Neill had undergone .....
    The NEXT word in the rewritten sentence is

    A. extraordinary B. existentialism C. rebelliousness
    D. spirituality E. a

14. Considering its great influence, Europe is surprisingly small.
    REWRITTEN:
    The smallness of Europe is surprising when one ...
    The NEXT word in the rewritten sentence is

    A. influences B. is C. considers
    D. knows E. consideration

15. Until late in the 1800's we knew nothing of a remarkable civilization which was old when the Greeks arrived.
    REWRITTEN:
    One remarkable civilization which was old when the Greeks arrived .....
    Somewhere in the part of the rewritten sentence indicated by dots is the word

    A. we B. unknown C. knew
    D. nothing E. of

16. Our knowledge of Aegean civilization comes largely from the work of two men.
    REWRITTEN:
    The work of two men ....
    The NEXT word in the rewritten sentence is

    A. comes B. teaches C. acknowledges
    D. enhances E. contributes

17. Twelve of the most important deities formed a council, which was supposed to meet on snowcapped Mount Olympus, in northern Thessaly.
    REWRITTEN:
    Mount Olympus, in northern Thessaly, was supposed to be the..........
    The NEXT word(s) in the rewritten sentence is (are)

    A. meeting place   B. council   C. most important
    D. epitome   E. deities

17.____

18. In the United States the states and local governments regulate the public schools and supply them with funds.
    REWRITTEN:
    Public schools in the United States are .....
    Somewhere in the part of the rewritten sentence indicated by dots is the word

    A. them   B. regulate   C. subsidized
    D. governed   E. supplied

18.____

19. The obstacle of distance was partly overcome by the invention of the steamship and the building of the Suez Canal.
    REWRITTEN:
    The invention of the steamship and the building of the Suez Canal helped
    Somewhere in the part of the rewritten sentence indicated by dots is the word

    A. was   B. overcoming   C. overcome
    D. partly   E. shorten

19.____

20. Although cotton has been used for cloth since ancient times, It was not known in England until the seventeenth century when the East India Company brought *calico* (named for Calicut) from India.
    REWRITTEN:
    When the East India Company brought *calico* (named for Calicut) from India in the seventeenth century, it was England's first .....
    Somewhere in the part of the rewritten sentence indicated by dots is the word

    A. known   B. knowledge   C. was
    D. although   E. until

20.____

21. In the eighteenth century weaving was still done on the hand loom.
    REWRITTEN:
    The hand loom .....
    Somewhere in the part of the rewritten sentence indicated by dots is the word

    A. done   B. on   C. for
    D. remained   E. weaves

21.____

22. When rubbed with wool, amber accumulates a charge of static electricity and will then attract small pieces of pith or paper.
    REWRITTEN:
    Small pieces of pith or paper can .....
    The NEXT word in the rewritten sentence is

    A. accumulate   B. be   C. attract
    D. charge   E. then

22.____

23. As a result of the Second World War, cities were devastated and millions were left homeless.
    REWRITTEN:
    The Second World War resulted .....
    Somewhere in the part of the rewritten sentence indicated by dots is the word

    A. leaving   B. devastating   C. were
    D. deprivation   E. devastated

24. With the growing urbanization and mechanization of modern life has come increasing recognition of the evils of drunkenness.
    REWRITTEN:
    The evils of drunkenness have become .....
    Somewhere in the part of the rewritten sentence indicated by dots is the word

    A. recognition   B. recognized   C. come
    D. increasing   E. increased

25. Chekhov dilutes the melodramatic pathos by qualifying our sympathy for the victims.
    REWRITTEN:
    The result of Chekhov's .....
    The *NEXT* word in the rewritten sentence is

    A. dilution   B. diluting   C. melodramatic
    D. qualification E. qualifying

KEYS (CORRECT ANSWERS)

1.	C	11.	D
2.	B	12.	B
3.	A	13.	E
4.	E	14.	C
5.	D	15.	B
6.	A	16.	E
7.	B	17.	A
8.	C	18.	E
9.	E	19.	C
10.	A	20.	D

21. C
22. B
23. A
24. B
25. E

6 (#1)

ACCEPTABLY REWRITTEN

1. Because its central figure conforms to the definitions of the mythic hero supplied by Northrup Frye, in THE ANATOMY OF CRITICISM, the messianic drama is <u>categorized</u> in the literary genre of myth or romance.

2. Julian is revealed <u>by</u> Ibsen to be a false Messiah, in THE EMPEROR JULIAN, the second part of the drama.

3. Because it is more <u>subtly</u> hidden, Chekhov's use of melodrama is more interesting.

4. Shaw responded to this with a partial <u>withdrawal</u> from his public concerns into a more personal, private, and, poetic form of expression.

5. He is <u>drawn</u> back again by life, against his will, in the form of uncontrollable instinct.

6. This drama is <u>unpopular</u> partly because it receives such destructive criticism when the modern world wants affirmations.

7. It is equally difficult for Shaw to accept the concept of a malevolent or determined man as it is <u>for him</u> to accept the concept of a determined and mindless universe.

8. Among the plant and animal microrganisms which we <u>know</u> that Leewen-hoek saw because of his descriptions, there may have been some bacteria.

9. The Russian fleet was quickly overcome by the Japanese <u>who</u> then landed troops on the mainland of Asia.

10. The movement <u>was</u> suppressed by an army of twenty thousand men sent by Napoleon who would not tolerate such an arrangement.

11. Marx realized that the success of the program <u>required</u> the united support of workingmen all over the world.

12. One reflection of <u>the poet's</u> deep belief in the closeness of nature to the human soul can be found in his beautiful descriptions of nature.

13. O'Neill had undergone <u>a</u> spiritual metamorphosis from a messianic into an existential rebel, of which this play is an extraordinary chronicle.

14. The smallness of Europe is surprising when one <u>considers</u> its great influence.

15. One remarkable civilization which was old when the Greeks arrived was <u>unknown</u> to us until late in the 1800's.

16. The work of two men <u>contributes</u> largely to our knowledge of Aegean civilization.

17. Snowcapped Mount Olympus, in northern Thessaly, was supposed to be the <u>meeting place</u> for a council formed by twelve of the most important deities.

18. Public schools in the United States are regulated and <u>supplied</u> with funds by the states and local government.

19. The invention of the steamship and the building of the Suez Canal helped to <u>overcome</u> the obstacle of distance.

20. When the East India Company brought *calico* (named for Calicut) from India in the seventeenth century, it was England's first introduction to cotton, <u>although</u> it has been used for cloth since ancient times.

21. The hand loom was still used <u>for</u> weaving in the eighteenth century.

22. Small pieces of pith or paper can <u>be</u> attracted by amber if it has been rubbed with wool to accumulate a charge of static electricity.

23. The Second World War resulted in the devastation of cities and the <u>leaving</u> homeless of millions.

24. The evils of drunkenness have become increasingly <u>recognized</u> with the growing urbanization and mechanization of modern life.

25. The result of Chekhov's <u>qualifying</u> our sympathy for the victims is the dilution of the melodramatic pathos.

TEST 2

1. While gazing through his microscope at a drop of water, he saw many kinds of creatures with one or a few cells, which wriggled about and devoured food.
   BEGIN THE SENTENCE WITH
       Many kinds of creatures with one or a few cells wriggling about .....
   Somewhere in the part of the rewritten sentence indicated by dots is (are) the word(s)

A. he saw	B. and devoured	C. which
D. by him	E. while gazing	

2. The worship of ancestors in China must have arisen in prehistoric times, judging from the reference to it in the most ancient Chinese literature.
   SUBSTITUTE
       ....since the most ancient Chinese literature for judging ...
   The *NEXT* words in the rewritten sentence are

A. the references	B. is judged	C. refers it
D. refers to	E. from the	

3. She divided the bread among them, without considering a share for herself.
   BEGIN THE SENTENCE WITH
       She did not .....
   Somewhere in the part of the rewritten sentence indicated by dots is(are) the word(s)

A. divided	B. when she	C. without
D. considering	E. dividing	

4. Since Smith has been a resident here for twenty years, we should give serious consideration to his suggestions.
   SUBSTITUTE
       ... seriously for give serious
   THE *NEXT* WORD(S) IN THE REWRITTEN SENTENCE IS (ARE)

A. to	B. consideration	C. consider
D. give consideration	E. would	

5. In the fight for women's suffrage one judge's decision had little effect, for the most part, upon the ladies' determination.
   CHANGE
       ...effect to effected
   Somewhere in the part of the rewritten sentence indicated by dots is (are) the word(s)

A. had	B. upon	C. part, upon
D. had, for	E. part, very little	

6. His approach to the committee was certainly not conducive to a cordial reception of his proposals, which were, at best, of doubtful validity.
   BEGIN THE SENTENCE WITH
       He approached .....
   Somewhere in the part of the rewritten sentence Indicated by dots is(are) the word(s)

A. was certainly	B. which was	C. to the
D. his	E. committee was	

7. When the thirsty horse had drunk its fill, it trotted briskly down the road.
   BEGIN THE SENTENCE WITH
   　　The thirsty horse ......
   The *NEXT* word(s) in the rewritten sentence is (are)

   A. having   B. it trotted   C. when
   D. had   E. had trotted

8. This country must either set up flood controls or be prepared to lose billions of dollars annually.
   BEGIN THE SENTENCE WITH
   　　If......
   Somewhere in the part of the rewritten sentence indicated by dots is (are) the word(s)

   A. either   B. must set   C. does not
   D. or   E. country must

9. They are not in Boston now, but I think they're going to that city next week.
   BEGIN THE SENTENCE WITH
   　　I think .....
   Somewhere in the part of the rewritten sentence indicated by dots is (are) the word(s)

   A. but I   B. in Boston   C. to Boston
   D. to that   E. now, but

10. Mt.Kinley, in Alaska, is higher than any other mountain in North America.
    INSERT THE WORD
    　　the after is .....
    The *NEXT* word in the rewritten sentence is

    A. highest   B. other   C. any
    D. than   E. higher

11. As a result of the Industrial Revolution, cities grew very rapidly and the demand for food and raw materials increased.
    BEGIN THE SENTENCE WITH
    　　A result .....
    Somewhere in the part of the rewritten sentence indicated by dots is (are) the word(s)

    A. grew   B. rapidly   C. the demand
    D. materials increased E. increased demand

12. Since the late eighteenth century, when the American and French revolutions took place, democracy has had a slow but persistent growth.
    SUBSTITUTE
    　　After for Since .....
    Somewhere in the part of the rewritten sentence indicated by dots is (are) the word(s)

    A. slow   B. has had   C. persistently
    D. growth   E. slow but persistent

13. The Treaty of Versailles placed the entire blame for World War I on Germany and her allies.
    BEGIN THE SENTENCE WITH
    　　Germany......
    Somewhere in the part of the rewritten sentence indicated by dots is the word

A. placed   B. on   C. blame
D. were   E. entire

14. A few years after Harvey's death, other scientists began to study the blood vessels with the aid of microscopes.
    BEGIN THE SENTENCE WITH
       Blood vessels .....
    Somewhere in the part of the rewritten sentence indicated by dots is (are) the word(s)

    A. by   B. began   C. study
    D. to   E. the study

15. This pamphlet is in response to requests of various groups for a more permanent and usable form of this material.
    BEGIN THE SENTENCE WITH
       To provide .....
    Somewhere in the part of the rewritten sentence indicated by dots is (are) the word(s)

    A. responding to   B. as a response to   C. requested
    D. in response to   E. requesting

16. The space science events chosen for development illustrate types of experiences in which mathematics and science have a mutually enhancing effect on each other.
    SUBSTITUTE
       ...are illustrated by for illustrate...
    Somewhere in the part of the rewritten sentence indicated by dots is(are) the word(s)

    A. have had   B. have   C. had had
    D. may be shown to have E. has

17. The criteria will be useful throughout the course in setting up specific objectives, providing learning experiences, and making periodic evaluations.
    SUBSTITUTE
       Use the criteria throughout the course for The criteria will be useful throughout the course ...
    The NEXT word in the rewritten sentence is

    A. in   B. for   C. to   D. with   E. by

18. The objectives of a training program are achieved by learning experiences designed to help the trainees develop those behaviors and abilities designated in the objectives.
    BEGIN THE SENTENCE WITH
       To achieve .....
    Somewhere in the part of the rewritten sentence indicated by dots is (are) the word(s)

    A. employ   B. to use   C. it will be useful
    D. create   E. to create

19. Because all of the suggested facilities will not be available in every community, it remains for the teacher to modify or supplement the following suggestions.
    BEGIN THE SENTENCE WITH
       The teacher .....
    The word that occurs IMMEDIATELY before the word *modify*, is

    A. could   B. might   C. would   D. must   E. should

20. Although teachers differ in their ways or organizing and coordinating important parts of their presentations, they agree that the purpose of a lesson is effective and meaningful classroom instruction.
BEGIN THE SENTENCE WITH
    Although teachers agree .....
The FIRST word of the main clause in the rewritten sentence is

    A. the   B. teachers   C. they   D. differing   E. it

21. Many common physical quantities such as temperature, the speed of a moving object, or the displacement of a ship can be expressed as a certain number of units.
BEGIN THE SENTENCE WITH
    One can express .....
The NEXT word(s) in the rewritten sentence is (are)

    A. as   B. many   C. in   D. a ship's   E. the

22. A parallel-tuned circuit, on the other hand, offers a very high impedance to currents of its natural, or resonant, frequency and a relatively low impedance to others.
BEGIN THE SENTENCE WITH
    A very high impedance .....
The NEXT words in the rewritten sentence are

    A. is offered to   B. offers to   C. is offered for
    D. is offered by   E. on the other hand

23. As the term implies, a voltage feedback amplifier transfers a voltage from the output of the amplifier back to its input.
CHANGE
    ... transfers to is transferred ...
The FIRST words of the rewritten sentence are

    A. A voltage
    B. Back to its input
    C. A voltage feedback amplifier
    D. In accordance with the term
    E. From the output

24. Unemployment among youth is a serious problem now, and unless the economy grows much more rapidly in the future than it has during the past decade, today's youngsters will feel the sharp pinch of declining ratios of new employment opportunities to persons seeking work.
BEGIN THE SENTENCE WITH
    Unless the economy grows, ...
The LAST CLAUSE in the rewritten sentence begins with

    A. today's   B. unemployment   C. and unless
    D. now   E. since

25. In a great society, talents are evoked and realized, creative minds probe the frontiers of knowledge, expectations of excellence are widely shared.
BEGIN THE SENTENCE WITH
    A great society .....
The NEXT words in the rewritten sentence are

A. evokes and realizes
B. talents, creative minds, and expectations of excellence
C. features
D. is characterized by
E. is one in which

KEYS (CORRECT ANSWERS)

1.	D	11.	E
2.	D	12.	C
3.	B	13.	D
4.	C	14.	A
5.	E	15.	D
6.	B	16.	B
7.	A	17.	C
8.	C	18.	A
9.	C	19.	E
10.	A	20.	C

21. A
22. E
23. A
24. E
25. E

ACCEPTABLY REWRITTEN

1. Many kinds of creatures with one or a few cells, wriggling about and devouring food, were seen <u>by him</u> while he was gazing through his microscope at a drop of water.

2. The worship of ancestors in China must have arisen in prehistoric times since the most ancient Chinese literature <u>refers to</u> it.

3. She did not consider a share for herself <u>when she</u> divided the bread among them.

4. Since Smith has been a resident here for twenty years, we should seriously <u>consider</u> his suggestions.

5. In the fight for women's suffrage one judge's decision affected the ladies' decision, for the most <u>part, very little.</u>

6. He approached the committee in a way which was certainly not conducive to a cordial reception of his proposals, which were, at best, of doubtful validity.

7. The thirsty horse, having drunk its fill, trotted briskly down the road.

8. If this country does not set up flood controls, it must be prepared to lose billions of dollars annually.

9. I think they're going to Boston next week, though they're not in that city now.

10. Mt.Kinley, in Alaska, is the highest mountain in North America.

11. A result of the Industrial Revolution was the very rapid growth of cities and the increased-demand for food and raw materials.

12. After the late eighteenth century, when the American and French revolutions took place, democracy grew slowly, but persistently.

13. Germany and her allies were blamed entirely for World War I by the Treaty of Versailles.

14. Blood vessels were studied by other scientists, with the aid of microscopes, a few years after Harvey's death.

15. To provide a more permanent and usable form of this material, in response to the requests of various groups, this pamphlet has been written.

16. The space science events chosen for development are illustrated by types of experiences in which mathematics and science have a mutually enhancing effect on each other.

17. Use the criteria throughout the course to set up specific objectives, provide learning experiences, and make periodic evaluations.

18. To achieve the objectives of a training program employ learning experiences designed to help the trainees develop those behaviors and abilities designated in the objectives.

19. The teacher should modify or supplement the following suggestions because all of the suggested facilities will not be available in every community.

20. Although teachers agree that the purpose of a lesson is effective and meaningful classroom instruction, they differ in their ways of organizing and coordinating important parts of their presentations.

21. One can express as a certain number of units many common physical quantities such as temperature, the speed of a moving object, or the displacement of a ship.

22. A very high impedance, on the other hand, is offered by a parallel-tuned circuit to currents of its natural, or resonant, frequency and a relatively low impedance to others.

23. A voltage is transferred from the output of the amplifier back to its input by a voltage feedback amplifier, as its name implies.

24. Unless the economy grows much more rapidly in the future than it has during the past decade, today's youngsters will feel the sharp pinch of declining ratios of new employment opportunities to persons seeking work <u>since</u> unemployment among youth is a serious problem now.

25. A great society <u>is one in which</u> talents are evoked and realized, creative minds probe the frontiers of knowledge, expectations of excellence are widely shared.

PREPARING WRITTEN MATERIAL

PARAGRAPH REARRANGEMENT
COMMENTARY

The sentences which follow are in scrambled order. You are to rearrange them in proper order and indicate the letter choice containing the correct answer at the space at the right.

Each group of sentences in this section is actually a paragraph presented in scrambled order. Each sentence in the group has a place in that paragraph; no sentence is to be left out. You are to read each group of sentences and decide upon the best order in which to put the sentences so as to form as well-organized paragraph.

The questions in this section measure the ability to solve a problem when all the facts relevant to its solution are not given.

More specifically, certain positions of responsibility and authority require the employee to discover connections between events sometimes, apparently, unrelated. In order to do this, the employee will find it necessary to correctly infer that unspecified events have probably occurred or are likely to occur. This ability becomes especially important when action must be taken on incomplete information.

Accordingly, these questions require competitors to choose among several suggested alternatives, each of which presents a different sequential arrangement of the events. Competitors must choose the MOST logical of the suggested sequences.

In order to do so, they may be required to draw on general knowledge to infer missing concepts or events that are essential to sequencing the given events. Competitors should be careful to infer only what is essential to the sequence. The plausibility of the wrong alternatives will always require the inclusion of unlikely events or of additional chains of events which are NOT essential to sequencing the given events.

It's very important to remember that you are looking for the best of the four possible choices, and that the best choice of all may not even be one of the answers you're given to choose from.

There is no one right way to these problems. Many people have found it helpful to first write out the order of the sentences, as they would have arranged them, on their scrap paper before looking at the possible answers. If their optimum answer is there, this can save them some time. If it isn't, this method can still give insight into solving the problem. Others find it most helpful to just go through each of the possible choices, contrasting each as they go along. You should use whatever method feels comfortable, and works, for you.

While most of these types of questions are not that difficult, we've added a higher percentage of the difficult type, just to give you more practice. Usually there are only one or two questions on this section that contain such subtle distinctions that you're unable to answer confidently, and you then may find yourself stuck deciding between two possible choices, neither of which you're sure about.

EXAMINATION SECTION
TEST 1

DIRECTIONS: Each group of sentences in this section is actually a paragraph presented in scrambled order. Each sentence in the group has a place in that paragraph; no sentence is to be left out. You are to read each group of sentences so as to form a well-organized paragraph. Before trying to answer the questions which follow each group of sentences, jot down the correct order of the sentences. Then answer each of the questions by printing the letter of the correct answer in the space at the right. Remember that you will receive credit only for answers marked.

- P. It is unfounded because, while the weak resent the power of the strong, they also respect it.
- Q. The hesitancy stems from a concern for public opinion in other countries.
- R. The United States has ordinarily been ill at ease in using its military power in support of its interests.
- S. The concern is largely unfounded.
- T. The roots of American hesitancy are deeply imbedded in the American mind.

1. Which sentence did you put last?
   A. P   B. Q   C. R   D. S   E. T

2. Which sentence did you put after Sentence R?
   A. P
   B. Q
   C. S
   D. T
   E. None of the above. Sentence R is last.

3. Which sentence did you put before Sentence S?
   A. P
   B. Q
   C. R
   D. T
   E. None of the above. Sentence S is first.

4. Which sentence did you put before Sentence R?
   A. P
   B. Q
   C. S
   D. T
   E. None of the above. Sentence R is last.

5. Which sentence did you put fourth?
   A. P   B. Q   C. R   D. S   E. T

KEY (CORRECT ANSWERS)

1. A
2. D
3. B
4. E
5. D

TEST 2

DIRECTIONS: Each group of sentences in this section is actually a paragraph presented in scrambled order. Each sentence in the group has a place in that paragraph; no sentence is to be left out. You are to read each group of sentences so as to form a well-organized paragraph. Before trying to answer the questions which follow each group of sentences, jot down the correct order of the sentences. Then answer each of the questions by printing the letter of the correct answer in the space at the right. Remember that you will receive credit only for answers marked.

P. Its lawlessness was virtually non-existent.
Q. The *Old West,* as portrayed in motion pictures, on television, and in books, is completely distorted.
R. It is obvious, therefore, that the *Old West* is falsely presented in mass media solely for commercial purposes.
S. Its heroes, too, were far from heroic.
T. Those who lived in the *Old West* in its final days, or talked to oldtimers, know the truth.

1. Which sentence did you put last?
   A. P   B. Q   C. R   D. S   E. T

2. Which sentence did you put after Sentence Q?
   A. P
   B. R
   C. S
   D. T
   E. None of the above. Sentence Q is last.

3. Which sentence did you put before Sentence S?
   A. P
   B. Q
   C. R
   D. T
   E. None of the above. Sentence S is first.

4. Which sentence did you put before Sentence Q?
   A. P
   B. R
   C. S
   D. T
   E. None of the above. Sentence Q is first.

5. Which sentence did you put after Sentence S?
   A. P
   B. Q
   C. R
   D. T
   E. None of the above. Sentence S is last.

KEY (CORRECT ANSWERS)

1. C
2. D
3. A
4. E
5. C

TEST 3

DIRECTIONS: Each group of sentences in this section is actually a paragraph presented in scrambled order. Each sentence in the group has a place in that paragraph; no sentence is to be left out. You are to read each group of sentences so as to form a well-organized paragraph. Before trying to answer the questions which follow each group of sentences, jot down the correct order of the sentences. Then answer each of the questions by printing the letter of the correct answer in the space at the right. Remember that you will receive credit only for answers marked.

P. One advertising executive became agitated recently when he suddenly realized that the floors of supermarkets were being unimaginatively used merely to walk on.
Q. Blank spaces, advertising men feel, cry out to be filled with merchandise-hustling messages.
R. He invented a slide projector which projects images on sheets of translucent plastic imbedded in supermarket floors.
S. At once, he got to work to correct this unforgiveable oversight.
T. As nature abhors a vacuum, so do advertising men decry blank spaces.

1. Which sentence did you put last?
   A. P
   B. Q
   C. B
   D. T
   E. None of the above. Sentence R is last.

2. Which sentence did you put third?
   A. P   B. Q   C. R   D. S   E. T

3. Which sentence did you put before Sentence T?
   A. P
   B. Q
   C. R
   D. T
   E. None of the above. Sentence T is first.

4. Which sentence did you put after Sentence P?
   A. Q
   B. R
   C. S
   D. T
   E. None of the above. Sentence P is last.

5. Which sentence did you put before Sentence Q?
   A. P
   B. R
   C. S
   D. T
   E. None of the above. Sentence Q is last.

KEY (CORRECT ANSWERS)

1. E
2. A
3. E
4. C
5. D

TEST 4

DIRECTIONS: Each group of sentences in this section is actually a paragraph presented in scrambled order. Each sentence in the group has a place in that paragraph; no sentence is to be left out. You are to read each group of sentences so as to form a well-organized paragraph. Before trying to answer the questions which follow each group of sentences, jot down the correct order of the sentences. Then answer each of the questions by printing the letter of the correct answer in the space at the right. Remember that you will receive credit only for answers marked.

P. It is estimated that Americans smoked almost a trillion cigarettes in 1966, while they smoked only several hundred million cigars and pipefuls of tobacco.
Q. Originally, they were considered exclusively a *ladies'* smoke.
R. Only in this century did cigarettes become popular in the United States.
S. Far more Americans smoke cigarettes today than smoke cigars and pipes combined.
T. This was not always the case, however.

1. Which sentence did you put first?
   A. P   B. Q   C. R   D. S   E. T

2. Which sentence did you put after Sentence Q?
   A. P
   B. R
   C. S
   D. T
   E. None of the above. Sentence Q is last.

3. Which sentence did you put before Sentence T?
   A. P
   B. Q
   C. R
   D. S
   E. None of the above. Sentence T is last.

4. Which sentence did you put after Sentence R?
   A. P
   B. Q
   C. S
   D. T
   E. None of the above. Sentence R is last.

5. Which sentence did you put before Sentence R?
   A. P
   B. Q
   C. S
   D. T
   E. None of the above. Sentence R is first.

KEY (CORRECT ANSWERS)

1. D
2. E
3. A
4. B
5. D

1. A
2. E
3. C
4. D
5. C

KEY (CORRECT ANSWERS)

1. A
2. C
3. C
4. E
5. B

PREPARING WRITTEN MATERIALS

EXAMINATION SECTION
TEST 1

DIRECTIONS: Each of the two sentences in the following questions may contain errors in punctuation, capitalization, or grammar.
If there is an error in only Sentence I, mark your answer A. If there is an error in only Sentence II, mark your answer B.
If there is an error in both Sentence I and Sentence II, mark your answer C. If both Sentence I and Sentence II are correct, mark your answer D.

1. I. The task of typing these reports is to be divided equally between you and me. 1.____
   II. If I was he, I would use a different method for filing these records.

2. I. The new clerk is just as capable as some of the older employees, if not more capable. 2.____
   II. Using his knowledge of arithmetic to check the calculations, the supervisor found no errors in the report.

3. I. A typist who does consistently superior work probably merits promotion. 3.____
   II. In its report on the stenographic unit, the committee pointed out that neither the stenographers nor the typists were adequately trained.

4. I. Entering the office, the desk was noticed immediately by the visitor. 4.____
   II. Arrangements have been made to give this training to whoever applies for it.

5. I. The office manager estimates that this assignment, which is to be handled by you and I, will require about two weeks for completion. 5.____
   II. One of the recommendations of the report is that these kind of forms be discarded because they are of no value.

6. I. The supervisor knew that the typist was a quiet, cooperative, efficient, employee. 6.____
   II. The duties of a stenographer are to take dictation notes at conferences and transcribing them.

7. I. The stenographer has learned that she, as well as two typists, is being assigned to the new unit. 7.____
   II. We do not know who you have designated to take charge of the new program.

8. I. He asked, "When do you expect to return?" 8.____
   II. I doubt whether this system will be successful here; it is not suitable for the work of our agency.

9. I. It is a policy of this agency to encourage punctuality as a good habit for we employees to adopt. 9.____
   II. The successful completion of the task was due largely to them cooperating effectively with the supervisor.

10. I. Mr. Smith, who is a very competent executive has offered his services to our department. 10.____
    II. Every one of the stenographers who work in this office is considered trustworthy.

11. I. It is very annoying to have a pencil sharpener, which is not in proper working order. 11.____
    II. The building watchman checked the door of Charlie's office and found that the lock has been jammed.

12. I. Since he went on the New York City council a year ago, one of his primary concerns has been safety in the streets. 12.____
    II. After waiting in the doorway for about 15 minutes, a black sedan appeared.

13. I. When you are studying a good textbook is important. 13.____
    II. He said he would divide the money equally between you and me.

14. I. The question is, "How can a large number of envelopes be sealed rapidly without the use of a sealing machine?" 14.____
    II. The administrator assigned two stenographers, Mary and I, to the new bureau.

15. I. A dictionary, in addition to the office management textbooks, were placed on his desk. 15.____
    II. The concensus of opinion is that none of the employees should be required to work overtime.

16. I. Mr. Granger has demonstrated that he is as courageous, if not more courageous, than Mr. Brown. 16.____
    II. The successful completion of the project depends on the manager's accepting our advisory opinion.

17. I. Mr. Ames was in favor of issuing a set of rules and regulations for all of us employees to follow. 17.____
    II. It is inconceivable that the new clerk knows how to deal with that kind of correspondence.

18. I. The revised referrence manual is to be used by all of the employees. 18.____
    II. Mr. Johnson told Miss Kent and me to accumulate all the letters that we receive.

19. I. The supervisor said, that before any changes would be made in the attendance report, there must be ample justification for them. 19.____
    II. Each of them was asked to amend their preliminary report.

20. I. Mrs. Peters conferred with Mr. Roberts before she laid the papers on his desk. 20.____
    II. As far as this report is concerned, Mr. Williams always has and will be responsible for its preparation.

KEY (CORRECT ANSWERS)

1. B
2. D
3. D
4. A
5. C

6. C
7. B
8. D
9. C
10. A

11. C
12. C
13. A
14. B
15. C

16. A
17. B
18. A
19. C
20. B

TEST 2

DIRECTIONS: Each question or incomplete statement is followed by several suggested answers or completions. Select the one that BEST answers the question or completes the statement. *PRINT THE LETTER OF THE CORRECT ANSWER IN THE SPACE AT THE RIGHT.*

Questions 1-9.

DIRECTIONS: Questions 1 through 9 consist of pairs of sentences which may or may not contain errors in grammar, capitalization, or punctuation.
If both sentences are correct, mark your answer A.
If the first sentence only is correct, mark your answer B.
If the second sentence only is correct, mark your answer C.
If both sentences are incorrect, mark your answer D.
NOTE: Consider a sentence correct if it contains no errors, although there may be other correct ways of writing the sentence.

1. I. An unusual conference will be held today at George Washington high school. 1.____
    II. The principal of the school, Dr. Pace, described the meeting as "a unique opportunity for educators to exchange ideas."

2. I. Studio D, which they would ordinarily use, will be occupied at that time. 2.____
    II. Any other studio, which is properly equipped, may be used instead.

3. I. D.H. Lawrence's <u>Sons and Lovers</u> were discussed on today's program. 3.____
    II. Either Eliot's or Yeats's work is to be covered next week.

4. I. This program is on the air for three years now, and has a well-established audience. 4.____
    II. We have received many complimentary letters from listeners, and scarcely no critical ones.

5. I. Both Mr. Owen and Mr. Mitchell have addressed the group. 5.____
    II. As has Mr. Stone, whose talks have been especially well received.

6. I. The original program was different in several respects from the version that eventually went on the air. 6.____
    II. Each of the three announcers who Mr. Scott thought had had suitable experience was asked whether he would be willing to take on the special assignment.

7. I. A municipal broadcasting system provides extensive coverage of local events, but also reports national and international news. 7.____
    II. A detailed account of happenings in the South may be carried by a local station hundreds of miles away.

8. I. Jack Doe the announcer and I will be working on the program. 8.____
    II. The choice of musical selections has been left up to he and I.

9. I. Mr. Taylor assured us that "he did not anticipate any difficulty in making arrangements for the broadcast ."
    II. Although there had seemed at first to be certain problems; these had been solved.

Questions 10-14.

DIRECTIONS: Questions 10 through 14 consist of pairs of sentences which may contain errors in grammar, sentence structure, punctuation, or spelling, or both sentences may be correct. Consider a sentence correct if it contains no errors, although there may be other correct ways of writing the sentence.
If only Sentence I contains an error, mark your answer A.
If only Sentence II contains an error, mark your answer B.
If both sentences contain errors, mark your answer C.
If both sentences are correct, mark your answer D.

10. I. No employee considered to be indispensable will be assigned to the new office.
    II. The arrangement of the desks and chairs give the office a neat appearance.

11. I. The recommendation, accompanied by a report, was delivered this morning.
    II. Mr. Green thought the procedure would facilitate his work; he knows better now.

12. I. Limiting the term "property" to tangible property, in the criminal mischief setting, accords with prior case law holding that only tangible property came within the purview of the offense of malicious mischief.
    II. Thus, a person who intentionally destroys the property of another, but under an honest belief that he has title to such property, cannot be convicted of criminal mischief under the Revised Penal Law.

13. I. Very early in its history, New York enacted statutes from time to time punishing, either as a felony or as a misdemeanor, malicious injuries to various kinds of property: piers, booms, dams, bridges, etc.
    II. The application of the statute is necessarily restricted to trespassory takings with larcenous intent: namely with intent permanently or virtually permanently to "appropriate" property or "deprive" the owner of its use.

14. I. Since the former Penal Law did not define the instruments of forgery in a general fashion, its crime of forgery was held to be narrower than the common law offense in this respect and to embrace only those instruments explicitly specified in the substantive provisions.
    II. After entering the barn through an open door for the purpose of stealing, it was closed by the defendants.

Questions 15-20.

DIRECTIONS: Questions 15 through 20 consist of pairs of sentences which may or may not contain errors in grammar, capitalization, or punctuation.
If both sentences are correct, mark your answer A.
If the first sentence only is correct, mark your answer B.
If the second sentence only is correct, mark your answer C.
If both sentences are incorrect, mark your answer D.

NOTE: Consider a sentence correct if it contains no errors, although there may be other correct ways of writing the sentence.

15. I. The program, which is currently most popular, is a news broadcast.
    II. The engineer assured his supervisor that there was no question of his being late again.

16. I. The announcer recommended that the program originally scheduled for that time be cancelled.
    II. Copies of the script may be given to whoever is interested.

17. I. A few months ago it looked like we would be able to broadcast the concert live.
    II. The program manager, as well as the announcers, were enthusiastic about the plan.

18. I. No speaker on the subject of education is more interesting than he.
    II. If he would have had the time, we would have scheduled him for a regular weekly broadcast.

19. I. This quartet, in its increasingly complex variations on a simple theme, admirably illustrates Professor Baker's point.
    II. Listeners interested in these kind of ideas will find his recently published study of Haydn rewarding.

20. I. The Commissioner's resignation at the end of next month marks the end of a long public service career.
    II. Outstanding among his numerous achievements were his successful implementation of several revolutionary schemes to reorganize the agency.

KEY (CORRECT ANSWERS)

1.	C	11.	D
2.	B	12.	C
3.	C	13.	B
4.	D	14.	A
5.	B	15.	C
6.	A	16.	A
7.	A	17.	D
8.	D	18.	B
9.	D	19.	B
10.	B	20.	B

ANSWER SHEET

TEST NO. _____ PART _____ TITLE OF POSITION _____
(AS GIVEN IN EXAMINATION ANNOUNCEMENT - INCLUDE OPTION, IF ANY)

PLACE OF EXAMINATION _____ (CITY OR TOWN) _____ (STATE) _____ DATE _____

RATING

USE THE SPECIAL PENCIL. MAKE GLOSSY BLACK MARKS.

	A	B	C	D	E		A	B	C	D	E		A	B	C	D	E		A	B	C	D	E		A	B	C	D	E
1						26						51						76						101					
2						27						52						77						102					
3						28						53						78						103					
4						29						54						79						104					
5						30						55						80						105					
6						31						56						81						106					
7						32						57						82						107					
8						33						58						83						108					
9						34						59						84						109					
10						35						60						85						110					

Make only ONE mark for each answer. Additional and stray marks may be counted as mistakes. In making corrections, erase errors COMPLETELY.

	A	B	C	D	E		A	B	C	D	E		A	B	C	D	E		A	B	C	D	E		A	B	C	D	E
11						36						61						86						111					
12						37						62						87						112					
13						38						63						88						113					
14						39						64						89						114					
15						40						65						90						115					
16						41						66						91						116					
17						42						67						92						117					
18						43						68						93						118					
19						44						69						94						119					
20						45						70						95						120					
21						46						71						96						121					
22						47						72						97						122					
23						48						73						98						123					
24						49						74						99						124					
25						50						75						100						125					

ANSWER SHEET

TEST NO. ______________ PART ______ TITLE OF POSITION ______________________________
(AS GIVEN IN EXAMINATION ANNOUNCEMENT - INCLUDE OPTION, IF ANY)

PLACE OF EXAMINATION ______________________________ (CITY OR TOWN) ______________ (STATE) DATE ______________

RATING

USE THE SPECIAL PENCIL. MAKE GLOSSY BLACK MARKS.

1 A B C D E	26 A B C D E	51 A B C D E	76 A B C D E	101 A B C D E
2 A B C D E	27 A B C D E	52 A B C D E	77 A B C D E	102 A B C D E
3 A B C D E	28 A B C D E	53 A B C D E	78 A B C D E	103 A B C D E
4 A B C D E	29 A B C D E	54 A B C D E	79 A B C D E	104 A B C D E
5 A B C D E	30 A B C D E	55 A B C D E	80 A B C D E	105 A B C D E
6 A B C D E	31 A B C D E	56 A B C D E	81 A B C D E	106 A B C D E
7 A B C D E	32 A B C D E	57 A B C D E	82 A B C D E	107 A B C D E
8 A B C D E	33 A B C D E	58 A B C D E	83 A B C D E	108 A B C D E
9 A B C D E	34 A B C D E	59 A B C D E	84 A B C D E	109 A B C D E
10 A B C D E	35 A B C D E	60 A B C D E	85 A B C D E	110 A B C D E

Make only ONE mark for each answer. Additional and stray marks may be counted as mistakes. In making corrections, erase errors COMPLETELY.

11 A B C D E	36 A B C D E	61 A B C D E	86 A B C D E	111 A B C D E
12 A B C D E	37 A B C D E	62 A B C D E	87 A B C D E	112 A B C D E
13 A B C D E	38 A B C D E	63 A B C D E	88 A B C D E	113 A B C D E
14 A B C D E	39 A B C D E	64 A B C D E	89 A B C D E	114 A B C D E
15 A B C D E	40 A B C D E	65 A B C D E	90 A B C D E	115 A B C D E
16 A B C D E	41 A B C D E	66 A B C D E	91 A B C D E	116 A B C D E
17 A B C D E	42 A B C D E	67 A B C D E	92 A B C D E	117 A B C D E
18 A B C D E	43 A B C D E	68 A B C D E	93 A B C D E	118 A B C D E
19 A B C D E	44 A B C D E	69 A B C D E	94 A B C D E	119 A B C D E
20 A B C D E	45 A B C D E	70 A B C D E	95 A B C D E	120 A B C D E
21 A B C D E	46 A B C D E	71 A B C D E	96 A B C D E	121 A B C D E
22 A B C D E	47 A B C D E	72 A B C D E	97 A B C D E	122 A B C D E
23 A B C D E	48 A B C D E	73 A B C D E	98 A B C D E	123 A B C D E
24 A B C D E	49 A B C D E	74 A B C D E	99 A B C D E	124 A B C D E
25 A B C D E	50 A B C D E	75 A B C D E	100 A B C D E	125 A B C D E